THE GRAND BUDAPEST HOTEL

THE GRAND BUDAPEST HOTEL

screenplay by
WES ANDERSON

story by
WES ANDERSON & HUGO GUINNESS

FABER & FABER

First published in 2014
by Faber & Faber Limited
Bloomsbury House
74–77 Great Russell Street
London WC1B 3DA

Typeset by Country Setting, Kingsdown, Kent CT14 8ES

A CIP record for this book
is available from the British Library

ISBN 978–0–571–31435–5

FSC
www.fsc.org
MIX
Paper from
responsible sources
FSC® C101712

2 4 6 8 10 9 7 5 3 1

CONTENTS

INTRODUCTION

by Hugo Guinness

I remember in Paris, 2007, Wes and I spent some time in restaurants and cafés and on walks in public parks discussing a mutual friend of ours. We talked about the things he said, his life, his mannerisms. He was an unusual character – full of anecdotes, charm, and *bon mots*.

He made us laugh.

Wes would write occasional casual notes about him. I then returned to New York and heard nothing from Wes about this character for five or six years. He was forgotten.

In 2012, out of the blue, Wes revived him.

We worked together over a period of several weeks and then multiple telephone calls. The character became M. Gustave H, the bisexual concierge of a hotel in middle Europe. A plot was devised around him, and dialogue was written, inch by inch. I would offer the occasional comment and answer Wes's hypothetical questions. If an idea or a line of dialogue by me actually got into the script, it was a good day. Mostly I just listened, and my suggestions were ignored. In a few short weeks, the script was finished, and Wes was off to East Germany to shoot *The Grand Budapest Hotel*.

FOOTNOTE

by Wes Anderson

Hugo has either deliberately or involuntarily distorted the above account of our collaboration.

I do not recall him ever being satisfied to see his suggestions ignored. He would, instead, become extremely moody and irritated in those instances, which usually makes him slightly funnier, and it's when he came up with some of our best bits.

Also, he is not inclined to sit back and listen. His instinct, I find, is to disagree and say something slightly belittling. His criticism is always insightful and pointed, not to say cruel, which helps it stick in the mind, often permanently. His contribution to this story should not be underestimated by anyone other than himself.

The Grand Budapest Hotel
was first shown at the Berlin Film Festival
in February 2014

Fox Searchlight Pictures in association with
Indian Paintbrush and Studio Babelsberg present

An American Empirical Picture

PRINCIPAL CAST

M. GUSTAVE	Ralph Fiennes
ZERO MOUSTAFA	Tony Revolori
MR. MOUSTAFA	Murray Abraham
SERGE X.	Mathieu Amalric
DMITRI	Adrien Brody
JOPLING	Willem Dafoe
DEPUTY KOVACS	Jeff Goldblum
LUDWIG	Harvey Keitel
YOUNG WRITER	Jude Law
M. IVAN	Bill Murray
HENCKELS	Edward Norton
AGATHA	Saoirse Ronan
M. JEAN	Jason Schwartzman
CLOTILDE	Léa Seydoux
MADAME D.	Tilda Swinton
AUTHOR	Tom Wilkinson
M. CHUCK	Owen Wilson

PRINCIPAL CREW

Directed by	Wes Anderson
Produced by	Wes Anderson, Scott Rudin, Steven Rales, Jeremy Dawson
Director of Photography	Robert Yeoman A.S.C.
Edited by	Barney Pilling
Production Designer	Adam Stockhausen
Costume Designer	Milena Canonero
Music by	Alexandre Desplat
Music Supervisor	Randall Poster
Special Photography Unit	Roman Coppola
Casting Directors	Douglas Aibel, Jina Jay

The Grand Budapest Hotel

EXT. CEMETERY. DAY

The present. A graveyard in the city center of a great Eastern European capital. Frost covers the ground among the stones and between rows of leafless trees. A teenage girl in a beret and trench-coat with a well-read, dog-eared novel called The Grand Budapest Hotel *tucked under her arm stands facing a tarnished bust of a slender, balding, spectacled old man. A bronze plaque below reads, in large letters:*

AUTHOR

Insert:

The plaque. There is a block of smaller text at the bottom which states simply:

IN MEMORY OF OUR NATIONAL TREASURE

All around the base of the statue there are little metal hooks, from which hang hundreds of hotel-room keys of every age and variety from all over the world. The girl adds a new set to the tribute.

INT. STUDY. DAY

Twenty years ago. A cluttered office with French windows and ornate mouldings. There are books in shelves and stacks, first editions, dictionaries, dime-store paperbacks, translations in numerous languages. There is a typewriter on the desk and an extensive collection of literary prizes on a bureau.

The author, seventy-five and identical to his sculpted image, sits with his hands clasped and addresses the camera.

AUTHOR

It is an extremely common mistake: people think the writer's imagination is always at work, that he is constantly inventing an endless supply of incidents and episodes, that

3

he simply dreams up his stories out of thin air. In point of fact, the opposite is true. Once the public knows you are a writer, they bring the characters and events to *you* – and as long as you maintain your ability to look and carefully listen, these stories will continue to seek you out –

A six-year-old boy dressed in a grey military uniform with short trousers appears next to the desk and points a miniature Luger pistol at the author. The author warns him, icy:

> AUTHOR
> Don't do it. Don't!

The boy hesitates, then fires. A yellow, plastic pellet ricochets off the author's chest and rings against a whiskey glass as the author makes a violent lunge for the boy – who evades him and dashes off. The author looks at a note card and rambles a bit, searching for his place.

> AUTHOR
> Over your lifetime. I can't tell you how many times. Somebody comes up to me. (*Back on track.*) To him who has often told the tales of others, many tales will be told.

The boy returns, the gun now tucked under his belt, and sits, immediately comfortable, on the author's lap with the old man's arms wrapped around his shoulders. The conflict seems never to have existed. They both look into the camera as the author concludes:

> AUTHOR
> The incidents that follow were described to me exactly as I present them here, and in a wholly unexpected way.

EXT. MOUNTAIN RANGE. DAY

The late sixties. A stunning view from a rusty, iron-lattice terrace suspended over a deep crevasse, green and lush, alongside a high cascade. The author continues in voice-over as the camera glides along a cracked path through a plot of untamed edelweiss and buttercups.

> AUTHOR
> (*voice-over*)
> A number of years ago, while suffering from a mild case of 'Scribe's Fever' (a form of neurasthenia common among

the intelligentsia of that time), I had decided to spend the month of August in the spa town of Nebelsbad below the Alpine Sudetenwaltz – and had taken up rooms in the Grand Budapest –

The camera comes to a stop as it reveals a sprawling nineteenth-century hotel and baths situated on a wide plateau. There is a deep, formidable staircase up to a regal entrance. There is a promenade above and a glass-panelled conservatory below. A rickety funicular groans as it slowly climbs its hillside tracks. The grass needs cutting, the roof needs patching, and more or less every surface of the building needs a coat of paint.

– a picturesque, elaborate, and once widely celebrated establishment. I expect some of you will know it. It was off-season and, by that time, decidedly out-of-fashion; and it had already begun its descent into shabbiness and eventual demolition.

Montage:

The nine other guests of the hotel each observed from a respectful distance: a frail student; a fat businessman; a burly hiker with a St. Bernard; a schoolteacher with her hair in a bun; a doctor; a lawyer; an actor; and so on.

AUTHOR
(*voice-over*)

What few guests we were had quickly come to recognize one another by sight as the only living souls residing in the vast establishment – although I do not believe any acquaintance among our number had proceeded beyond the polite nods we exchanged as we passed in the Palm Court and the Arabian Baths and on board the Colonnade Funicular. We were a very reserved group, it seemed – and, without exception, solitary.

Cut to:

An enormous, half-abandoned dining room. There are two hundred tables and fifty chandeliers. The ten guests sit, each on his or her own, at their separate tables, widely spaced across the giant restaurant.

A waiter carries a tray a great distance to the schoolteacher and serves her a plate of peas.

INT. LOBBY. EVENING

There are faded couches, fraying armchairs, and coffee tables with new, plastic tops. The carpets are threadbare, and the lighting in each area is either too dim or too bright. A concierge with a crooked nose smokes a cigarette as he lingers behind his desk. He is M. Jean.

(Note: the staff of the hotel in both the relevant time periods wear similar versions of the same purple uniform – while the public spaces reflect a cycle of 'regime changes'.)

On the wall behind M. Jean, there is a beautiful Flemish painting of a pale, young boy holding a piece of golden fruit. This is 'Boy with Apple'. A patch of water damage above seeps dangerously close to the picture-frame.

*The author (a fictionalized version of himself) wanders into the room
with his hands in his pockets. He has dark circles under his eyes.*

AUTHOR
(*voice-over*)
Perhaps as a result of this general silence, I had established
a casual and bantering familiarity with the hotel's concierge,
a west-continental known only as M. Jean, who struck one
as being, at once, both lazy and, really, quite accommodating.

*M. Jean quickly stubs out his cigarette as the author approaches – and
tucks the butt into his coat pocket.*

AUTHOR
(*voice-over*)
I expect he was not well-paid.

*The author and M. Jean chat amicably as they study a pamphlet of
Alpine tourist sites.*

In any case, one evening, as I stood conferring elbow-to-elbow with M. Jean, as had become my habit, I noticed a new presence in our company.

At the far end of the lobby, beyond Reception, a dark-skinned, white-haired seventy-year-old man in a three-piece-suit sits alone smoking a pipe. He is Mr. Moustafa.

AUTHOR
(*voice-over*)

A small, elderly man, smartly dressed, with an exceptionally lively, intelligent face – and an immediately perceptible air of sadness. He was, like the rest of us, alone – but also, I must say, he was the first that struck one as being, deeply and truly, lonely (a symptom of my own medical condition, as well).

Mr. Moustafa takes a sip of sherry. The author lowers his voice and asks discreetly:

AUTHOR
(*voice-over*)

'Who's this interesting, old fellow?' I inquired of M. Jean. To my surprise, he was distinctly taken aback. 'Don't you *know?*' he asked. 'Don't you *recognize* him?' He did look familiar. 'That's Mr. Moustafa himself! He arrived early this morning.'

The author looks to Mr. Moustafa again. Mr. Moustafa is now staring directly back at the author. The author quickly looks away and examines a detail in the woodwork on the ceiling.

This name will, no doubt, be familiar to the more seasoned persons among you. Mr. Zero Moustafa was, at one time, the richest man in Zubrowka; and was still, indeed, the owner of the Grand Budapest. 'He often comes and stays a week or more, three times a year, at least – but never in the season.' M. Jean signaled to me, and I leaned closer. 'I'll tell you a secret. He takes only a single-bed sleeping-room without a bath in the rear corner of the top floor – and it's smaller than the service elevator!'

The author seems genuinely intrigued by this information. He nods thoughtfully.

It was well-known: Moustafa had purchased and famously inhabited some of the most lavish castles and palazzos on the continent – yet, here, in his own, nearly empty hotel, he occupied a servant's quarters?

M. Jean frowns. The fat businessman, sitting at a table in the middle of the lobby drinking hot chocolate and eating biscotti, appears to be choking to death.

At that moment the curtain rose on a parenthetical, domestic drama which required the immediate and complete attention of M. Jean –

M. Jean dashes out from behind his desk. As he performs an improvised version of the Heimlich maneuver on the fat businessman, the German hiker enters the lobby with his St. Bernard. The rescue dog, sensing a human in distress, charges avidly, hurdling three tables and jostling the dessert cart, and arrives at the fat businessman's side just as a significant hunk of biscotti rockets out of his mouth, into the air, and lands on a saucer at the next table. M. Jean immediately detaches a cask hanging from the dog's neck, pours a generous shot of brandy into a water glass, and forces it down the fat businessman's throat.

– but, frankly, did not hold mine for long.

The other guests of the hotel begin to gather around the gasping victim as the author makes his way into the elevator. He presses a button, and the doors close.

Montage:

The author appears pensive as he: lies in bed that night staring up at the ceiling; sits in the dining room at breakfast eating toast and gazing into space; and floats through the conservatory ignoring flora at noon. He nods to the schoolteacher sketching an orchid. She smiles and nods back.

AUTHOR
(voice-over)
However, this premature intermission in the story of the curious old man had left me, as the expression goes,

gespannt wie ein Flitzebogen, that is, on the edge of my seat – where I remained throughout the next morning until, in what I have found to be its mysterious and utterly reliable fashion, fate, once again, intervened on my behalf.

INT. SPA. DAY

A steamy, underground mineral baths. Miniature tiles of various shapes and intricate patterns cover every inch of the walls, floors, and ceiling. Distant voices echo faintly through succeeding chambers.

A long row of identical, adjacent cubicles, each containing a blue tub and tiled in a more recent, utilitarian style. The author soaks. He shakes salts from a carton into the water and stirs it.

A voice interrupts from off-screen:

> MR. MOUSTAFA
> (*out of shot*)
> I admire your work.

The author hesitates. He looks around. He is not sure which general direction the voice came from.

> AUTHOR
> I beg your pardon?

> MR. MOUSTAFA
> (*out of shot*)
> I said, I know and admire your wonderful work.

There is a small splash, and Mr. Moustafa leans into view from behind a partition where he himself is soaking in a cubicle three tubs over. He wears a bathing cap. The author sits up straight and says formally:

> AUTHOR
> Thank you most kindly, sir.

> MR. MOUSTAFA
> (*teasing slightly*)
> Did M. Jean have a word or two to share with you about the aged proprietor of this establishment?

AUTHOR
(*reluctantly*)
I must confess, sir, I did, myself, inquire about you.

MR. MOUSTAFA
(*resigned*)
He's perfectly capable, of course, M. Jean – but we can't claim he's a first- or, in earnest, even second-rate concierge. (*Sadly.*) But there it is. Times have changed.

The author nods, attentive. He changes the subject to observe encouragingly, motioning toward the plunging pool across the hall:

AUTHOR
The thermal baths are very beautiful.

MR. MOUSTAFA
(*gently*)
They *were*, in their first condition. It couldn't be maintained, of course. Too decadent for current tastes – but I love it all, just the same. This enchanting old ruin.

Mr. Moustafa looks wistfully around the vaulted space. The author squints, holds up a finger, and asks gingerly:

AUTHOR
How did you come to buy it, if I may ask? The Grand Budapest?

Pause. Mr. Moustafa disappears back behind the partition. The author looks slightly puzzled. Mr. Moustafa immediately reappears, but he has turned himself around in the tub and is now facing the opposite direction so he can more comfortably rest in view. He props his elbow onto the edge of the bath. His eyes twinkle as he says:

MR. MOUSTAFA
I didn't.

At this moment, one of the matrons of the hammam blasts the fat, now naked, businessman with a jet of icy water. He hollers as he is sprayed down. Silence.

Mr. Moustafa and the author look back to each other. Each has raised an eyebrow. They both smile slightly.

MR. MOUSTAFA

If you're not merely being polite (and you must tell me if that's the case), but if it genuinely does interest you: may I invite you to dine with me tonight, and it will be my pleasure and, indeed, my privilege to tell you – 'my' story. Such as it is.

INT. DINING ROOM. NIGHT

The enormous restaurant as before – but now one of the tables has been set for two and is occupied by the author and Mr. Moustafa. The nine other guests watch, curious, from their usual spots.

Mr. Moustafa stares at the wine list as he rattles off a robust order (oysters, soup, rabbit, fowl, lamb). 'Boy with Apple' is on the cover of the menu. The waiter departs.

MR. MOUSTAFA

That should provide us ample time – if I commence promptly.

AUTHOR

By all means.

Another waiter arrives to uncork a split of champagne and pours a thimbleful. Mr. Moustafa tastes it and nods. The waiter pours two full coupes. They each drink a long sip. Finally, Mr. Moustafa settles in:

MR. MOUSTAFA

It begins, as it must, with our mutual friend's predecessor. The beloved, *original* concierge of the Grand Budapest. (*With deep affection.*) It begins, of course, with –

Title:

PART 1: 'M. GUSTAVE'

INT. SITTING ROOM. DAY

The early thirties. A double-reception salon with high ceilings and two couches. There are six trunks and eight suitcases arranged neatly at the side of the room. Each is painted with the initials 'Mdm. C. V. D. u. T.' Outside, a light snow falls.

A tall, blond, forty-year-old concierge stands patiently alone surveying the room. He is tranquil, perfectly composed, waiting. He wears the faintest hint of mascara. He is M. Gustave.

M. Gustave crosses swiftly to the door and opens it just as a contingent of hotel staff arrives together from down the corridor. There are two waiters, two footmen, two bellboys, and an Arab teenager, small, cheerful, and alert, who appears to be some kind of page. He is Zero.

One of the waiters carries a table, and one carries a breakfast tray. M. Gustave ushers them in:

M. GUSTAVE

Bring the table to the window.

FIRST WAITER

Yes, M. Gustave.

M. GUSTAVE

Bring the tray to the table.

SECOND WAITER

Right away, M. Gustave.

M. GUSTAVE
(pointing to two hats)

Have those been brushed and blocked?

FOOTMAN

Of course, M. Gustave.

M. GUSTAVE

Pack them in the hat boxes. (*Pointing to a shopping bag.*) Is that from Oberstdorf and Company?

BELLBOY

I believe so, M. Gustave.

M. GUSTAVE

Second trunk. Who has the tickets?

Zero raises his hand.

ZERO

I do, M. Gustave.

M. GUSTAVE

Give them to me.

Zero hands M. Gustave a set of train tickets. M. Gustave studies them carefully. He nods and points.

These are in order. Wait in the corner.

Zero retreats. M. Gustave strides to the bedroom door, raps on it briefly, then swings it open.

Good morning, Madame. Your breakfast is served. The sitting room is a battlefield at the moment, but rest assured, you will be *en route* in precisely – (*Checks his watch.*) eleven minutes. You look heavenly. Pray be seated.

An immaculately dressed, eighty-year-old woman emerges from the bedroom, nimble, brisk – and highly agitated. She is Madame D. She is followed by two young women, a lady's maid and a private secretary, who quickly join the hubbub fidgeting with trunks and rushing to-and-fro preparing for their departure.

M. Gustave waits for Madame D. to sit, then joins her; at which point, she immediately leans across to him and says in a gravely serious, urgent whisper:

MADAME D.

I'm not leaving.

M. GUSTAVE
(*puzzled*)

Why not?

MADAME D.

I'm frightened.

M. GUSTAVE

Of what?

MADAME D.
I feel this may be the last time we ever see each other.

M. GUSTAVE
Why on earth would that be the case?

MADAME D.

I can't put it into words – but I *feel* it.

M. GUSTAVE

Well, for goodness' sake, there's no reason for you to leave
us if –

MADAME D.

Is there a priest in the hotel?

M. GUSTAVE

Of course not.

MADAME D.

There should be. I've always said so.

M. GUSTAVE

Well, I've always profoundly disagreed. The Grand Budapest
is no place for clergy.

MADAME D.

Come with me.

*M. Gustave hesitates slightly. He gestures to the tickets and speculates
in disbelief:*

M. GUSTAVE

To Lutz?

MADAME D.
(*desperately*)

Please.

M. GUSTAVE
(*wildly frustrated*)

How can I? With this enormous rock-pile around my neck
like an albatross. (*Taking charge.*) Tell me right now –
wholly, specifically, and without abbreviation: what's
troubling you? (*Surprised.*) Are you weeping?

*Tears have begun to stream down Madame D.'s cheeks. M. Gustave
produces a dazzling pink handkerchief and dries her eyes. The old
woman takes a deep breath.*

MADAME D.

Let us pray.

Madame D. closes her eyes, lowers her chin, and crosses herself. M. Gustave reluctantly follows suit. Silence. Madame D. snaps one eye back open suddenly:

MADAME D.

Well?

M. GUSTAVE
(*surprised*)

You want *me* to do it?

MADAME D.
(*with authority*)

If you don't mind.

M. GUSTAVE
(*instantly*)

Dear heavenly Father, please, protect our cherished guest as she travels through snow and sleet and under shadow of darkness. Guide her in the night to her final destination. Indeed, whatever luxury she may require, be it small or more extravagant, please, do grant –

MADAME D.
(*now with both eyes open*)

That's not a proper prayer.

M. GUSTAVE

Give me your hand.

Madame D. does so. M. Gustave firmly clasps it. He says in an affectionate, reassuring, patronizing voice:

M. GUSTAVE

You've nothing to fear. You're always anxious before you travel. I admit you appear to be suffering a more acute attack on this occasion, but, truly and honestly – (*Suddenly taken aback.*) Dear God. What've you done to your fingernails?

Madame D. wears an understated, pale-pink polish. She stiffens.

MADAME D.

I beg your pardon?

M. GUSTAVE

This diabolical varnish. The color's completely wrong.

MADAME D.
(*slightly uncertain*)

Really? You don't *like* it?

M. GUSTAVE

It's not that I don't like it. I'm physically repulsed. (*Checks his watch again.*) Time to go!

INT. CORRIDOR. DAY

The procession of trunks, cases, and assistants goes in one direction, and M. Gustave, Madame D., and Zero (carrying a small leather jewel case) go in the other.

Cut to:

The elevator on its way down. M. Gustave sits with Madame D. (now wearing gloves) on a velvet-upholstered bench. She clutches his arm and looks deeply concerned. Zero with the jewel case stands at attention alongside a veteran elevator operator.

M. GUSTAVE

Perhaps this will soothe you.

MADAME D.
(*alarmed*)

What? Don't recite.

M. GUSTAVE

Just listen to the words.

MADAME D.
(*anxious*)

Please. Not now.

M. GUSTAVE

Hush! (*Declaiming gently.*) 'While questing once in noble wood of grey, medieval pine, I came upon a tomb,

rain-slick'd, rubbed-cool, ethereal; its inscription long-vanished, yet still within its melancholy fissures –'

Madame D. sighs deeply yet does seem to calm somewhat as she accepts the inevitability of these stanzas.

EXT. FRONT ENTRANCE. DAY

The trunks are piled on the roof of a long, silver limousine. More suitcases stick out of the rumble seat (along with the two bellboys). Madame D. and her secretary sit inside the car. M. Gustave reaches in the window and tightens a fur stole around Madame D.'s shoulders.

MADAME D.
Will you light a candle for me, please? In the sacristy at Santa Maria.

Madame D. digs a five-Klubeck coin out of her handbag and presses it into M. Gustave's hand. He accepts it:

M. GUSTAVE
I'll see to it myself immediately. (*Saintly.*) Remember: I'm always with you.

M. Gustave begins to withdraw, but Madame D. grips his shoulder tightly. She whispers, sincere and impassioned, what she fears will be their last communication:

MADAME D.
I love you.

M. GUSTAVE
(*as if to a child*)
I love *you.*

(*Barking at the driver.*) Abfahren!

The driver hits the gas. M. Gustave watches as the vehicle races away, spitting ice-chips off the packed snow. Zero lingers outside the front door. M. Gustave says with discreet pride as he continues to stare off down the road into the village of Nebelsbad:

M. GUSTAVE
It's quite a thing winning the loyalty of a woman like that for nineteen consecutive seasons.

Zero hesitates – uncertain that he is, in fact, being addressed. He ventures:

> ZERO

Yes, sir.

> M. GUSTAVE

She's very fond of me, you know.

> ZERO

Yes, sir.

> M. GUSTAVE

I've never seen her like that before.

> ZERO

No, sir.

> M. GUSTAVE
> (*mildly concerned*)

She was shaking like a shitting dog.

> ZERO
> (*unfamiliar with the expression*)

Truly.

M. Gustave holds out the five-Klubeck coin, still staring off into the distance, and says rapidly, though distracted:

> M. GUSTAVE

Run to the cathedral of Santa Maria Christiana in Brucknerplatz. Buy one of the plain, half-length candles and take back four Klubecks in change. Light it in the sacristy, say a brief rosary, then go to Mendl's and get me a Courtesan *au chocolat*. If there's any money left, give it to the crippled shoeshine boy.

M. Gustave points to a blind child in leg braces crouched at the top of the funicular tracks. The boy whistles a war march while he polishes a man's boots.

> ZERO

Right away, sir.

Zero nods briskly and takes the coin. M. Gustave looks squarely at him for the first time.

> M. GUSTAVE

Hold it.

Zero freezes, poised to dash off. M. Gustave frowns slightly. He says finally, pointing:

> M. GUSTAVE

Who are you?

> ZERO
> (*stammering*)

Zero, sir. The new lobby boy.

> M. GUSTAVE
> (*mystified*)

Zero, you say?

> ZERO

Yes, sir.

> M. GUSTAVE

Well, I've never heard of you. I've never laid eyes on you. Who hired you?

> ZERO
> (*worried*)

Mr. Mosher, sir.

> M. GUSTAVE
> (*sharply*)

Mr. Mosher!

M. Gustave snaps his fingers. A man with neat, oily hair and a thin moustache briskly approaches. He is Mr. Mosher.

> MR. MOSHER

Yes, M. Gustave?

> M. GUSTAVE

Am I to understand you've surreptitiously hired this young man in the position of a lobby boy?

> MR. MOSHER

He's been engaged for a trial period – pending your approval, of course.

M. GUSTAVE
(*vaguely remembering*)
Perhaps. Thank you, Mr. Mosher.

MR. MOSHER
You're most welcome, M. Gustave.

M. Gustave looks back to Zero. He says ominously:

M. GUSTAVE
You're now going to be officially interviewed.

INT. LOBBY. DAY

M. Gustave strides through the front doors. Zero is quickly at his heels, terrified. M. Gustave withdraws a small notebook from his pocket as they walk. Zero asks, uncertain:

ZERO
Should I go and light the candle first?

M. GUSTAVE
(*not sure what he means*)
What? No. (*Starting the interview.*) Experience?

ZERO
(*anxious, very formal*)
Hotel Kinski, kitchen boy, six months. Hotel Berlitz, mop and broom boy, three months. Before that I was a skillet scrubber in the banquet hall at –

M. GUSTAVE
(*noting this*)
Experience: zero.

At this moment, a criss-crossing group of people simultaneously engage M. Gustave all at once. They are: a man in a finely tailored business suit with a pair of opera tickets in his hand, a doorman in a long coat holding a bouquet of white roses, and a tiny bellboy (this is Anatole).

HOTEL GUEST NO. I
Thank you again, M. Gustave.

M. GUSTAVE
(*curtly to Anatole*)
Straighten that cap, Anatole. (*Warmly to the hotel guest.*) The
pleasure is mine, Herr Schneider.

ANATOLE
(*working on it*)
The damn strap's busted.

M. GUSTAVE
(*studying the roses*)
These are not acceptable.

DOORMAN
I agree, M. Gustave.

*Suddenly, M. Gustave and Zero are alone again. M. Gustave resumes
his interrogation as they proceed across the carpet:*

M. GUSTAVE
Education?

ZERO
(*worried*)
I studied reading and spelling. I completed my primary
school certificate. I almost started –

M. GUSTAVE
(*noting this*)
Education: zero.

*A second criss-crossing group of people now engage M. Gustave. This
time: a very old Washroom Attendant carrying a monkey-wrench, the
head waiter wearing an apron and waving a menu, and a woman of
a certain age in a beautifully embroidered dress with a small dachshund
cradled in her arms.*

WASHROOM ATTENDANT
Now it's exploded.

M. GUSTAVE
(*sweetly to the dachshund*)
Good morning, Cicero. (*Coldly to the Washroom Attendant.*)
Call the goddamn plumber.

HOTEL GUEST NO. 2
(*flirtatious*)
This afternoon, M. Gustave?

HEAD WAITER
(*angrily*)
What in the hell is this?

M. GUSTAVE
(*equally flirtatious*)
Without fail, Frau Liebling. (*Sharply to the Head Waiter.*)
Not *now*!

The second interruption ends. M. Gustave continues:

M. GUSTAVE
Family?

ZERO
(*long pause*)
Zero.

M. GUSTAVE
(*noting this*)
I see.

M. Gustave leads Zero through a rotunda, below a grand, winding staircase, and back into the elevator. He closes his notebook. The elevator operator awaits instruction.

M. GUSTAVE
Six.

The elevator operator throws a lever and they begin to ascend. M. Gustave locks eyes with Zero.

M. GUSTAVE
Why do you want to be a lobby boy?

The elevator operator casts a sideways look. Zero searches for the honest answer – then finds it:

                          ZERO
Well, who *wouldn't* – at the Grand Budapest, sir? It's an
institution.

                      M. GUSTAVE
                   (*deeply impressed*)
Very good.

INT. SITTING ROOM. DAY

*M. Gustave and Zero re-enter Madame D.'s suite. M. Gustave walks
directly over to a pedestal where an envelope waits tucked beneath a
vase. He tears it open and withdraws a letter and a stack of bills
folded in half. He counts the money and says coolly:*

                      M. GUSTAVE
A thousand Klubecks.

                          ZERO
                      (*astonished*)
My goodness.

*M. Gustave skims the letter. He holds it up for Zero to see. There is a
lipstick-kiss at the bottom of the text. Zero is unsure how to interpret
this. M. Gustave raises his eyebrows and tucks the note and the bills
inside his jacket. His eyes glaze over in a moment of reverie. He sighs.
Zero makes a sudden realization:*

                          ZERO
Were *you* ever a lobby boy, sir?

                      M. GUSTAVE
                  (*bristling but playful*)
What do *you* think?

                          ZERO
                      (*speculative*)
Well, I suppose you had to start –

                      M. GUSTAVE
Go light the goddamn candle.

Title:

ONE MONTH LATER

INT. LOBBY. DAY

The crowded room buzzes in all corners. Zero circulates among tables and sofas holding up a folded telegram while he calls out a name, searching. A military officer in a grey uniform hails him, and Zero dashes over to deliver the missive.

> MR. MOUSTAFA
> (*voice-over*)
> And so, my life began. Junior lobby boy (in training), Grand Budapest Hotel, under the strict command of M. Gustave H. I became his pupil, and he was to be my counselor and guardian.

> M. GUSTAVE
> (*voice-over, rhetorical*)
> What is a lobby boy?

Montage:

Zero pushes an old man in a wheelchair. Zero arranges a white bouquet. Zero replaces dirty ashtrays, rearranges furniture, and shields a large woman with a toothpick from view as she excavates between her teeth.

> M. GUSTAVE
> (*voice-over*)
> A lobby boy is completely invisible, yet always in sight. A lobby boy remembers what people hate. A lobby boy anticipates the client's needs *before* the needs are needed. A lobby boy, above all, is discreet, to a fault.

Cut to:

M. Gustave, accompanied by Zero, advancing down a corridor at high velocity. On the floor next to each door they pass, a pair of shoes waits to be polished.

> M. GUSTAVE
> Our guests know their deepest secrets, some of which are,

frankly, rather unseemly, will go with us to our graves – so
keep your mouth shut, Zero.

                    ZERO
Yes, sir.

M. Gustave stops at the end of the hallway in front of a door labeled
KAISER FREDERICK SUITE. *He says to Zero:*

                  M. GUSTAVE
That's all for now.

Zero hesitates for an instant, then nods and reverses rapidly away.
M. Gustave withdraws a ring of pass-keys from his pocket. He looks
up and down the corridor furtively.

                 MR. MOUSTAFA
                  (*voice-over*)
I began to realize that many of the hotel's most valued and
distinguished guests – came for *him.*

Zero looks back briefly over his shoulder as he starts down the
staircase and sees M. Gustave slip into the suite. The door locks.

                 MR. MOUSTAFA
                  (*voice-over*)
It seemed to be an essential part of his duties, but I believe
it was also his pleasure.

Montage:

A succession of dames *of varying* grandeurs *seen tête-à-tête with*
M. Gustave: a sixty-year-old Russian chats with him in the tea salon;
a sixty-five-year-old German strolls with him on the promenade; a
seventy-year-old Argentinian shares a cigarette with him, naked in her
bed; a seventy-five-year-old Englishwoman washes his back in her
bath; and an eighty-year-old Austrian wearing a hairnet and a
nightgown gives him a blow-job while he watches in the mirror and
eats grapes. There is a platinum wig on a stand on the dressing table.

                 MR. MOUSTAFA
                  (*voice-over*)
The requirements were always the same. They had to be:
rich, old, insecure, vain, superficial, blonde, needy.

Cut to:

Mr. Moustafa and the author at their dinner table. The remains of a rabbit tart are replaced by a sizeable roasted pheasant as the author gently inquires:

> AUTHOR
>
> Why blonde?

> MR. MOUSTAFA
> *(after a moment's reflection)*
>
> Because they all *were*.

INT. ELEVATOR. DAY

M. Gustave, somewhat tousled, with lipstick on his cheek, stands waiting to arrive at his floor. He checks the railings for dust. The car stops and the elevator operator opens the gate. M. Gustave exits with a curt nod. A middle-aged couple enter.

> MR. MOUSTAFA
> *(voice-over)*
>
> He was, by the way, the most liberally perfumed man I had ever encountered. The scent announced his approach from a great distance and lingered for many minutes after he was gone.

As the elevator descends, the middle-aged couple sniffs the air. The man looks irritated. The woman swoons slightly.

INT. STAFF QUARTERS. MORNING

Zero wakes up in the pitch black in a tiny room smaller than a service elevator, turns on the light, springs to his feet dressed in white pajamas with short trousers, splashes water from a bowl onto his face, then quickly dampens and combs his hair. His uniform hangs neatly from a peg on the wall. He carefully grooms it with a clothes-brush.

> MR. MOUSTAFA
> *(voice-over)*
>
> I worked six days each week plus a half-day Sunday, five a.m. until just after midnight. Our meals were small but

frequent (for stamina): two breakfasts, two lunches, and a late supper. M. Gustave also delivered a nightly sermon.

INT. MESS HALL. NIGHT

The evening meal. Most of the hotel staff occupy a long table set for fifty. A thin, grey broth is served with boiled potatoes. M. Gustave starts at a little podium, then paces back and forth in front of it as he addresses the group. They begin to eat hungrily – but, at the same time, they continue to listen, attentive and respectful.

M. GUSTAVE

Rudeness is merely the expression of fear. People *fear* they won't get what they want. The most dreadful and unattractive person: only needs to be *loved* – and they will open up like a flower. I'm reminded of a verse. (*Reciting.*) 'The painter's brush touched the inchoate face by ends of nimble bristles – and, with that blush of first color, rendered her lifeless cheek, living; though languish—'

34

As the poetry begins, some of the diners' eye glaze over and there are faint sighs. Mr. Moustafa continues his narration:

> MR. MOUSTAFA
> (*voice-over*)
> His own dinner, he took alone in his room.

Cut to:

M. Gustave seated at a folding table in a room nearly identical to Zero's but with a connecting sitting room and kitchenette. He wears his uniform trousers and a white undershirt. He eats a bowl of cereal while listening to classical music on a radio set.

There are approximately twenty-five identical bottles of cologne on a shelf above the sink in the background. Each is labeled 'L'Air de Panache: *Pure Musk.'*

EXT. FRONT ENTRANCE. DAY

A large sedan with tire-chains arrives through the snow and parks in front of the hotel. A sign next to five stars on the side of the hood reads: GRAND BUDAPEST HOTEL. *One of the back doors opens, and a tall man in a double-breasted suit emerges. He carries a briefcase and wears a pointy beard. He is Deputy Kovacs. He hurries to the top of the steps where M. Gustave waits to greet him.*

> MR. MOUSTAFA
> (*voice-over*)
> The identity of the owner of the hotel was unknown to all of us. Each month, his emissary, known as Deputy Kovacs, arrived to review the books and convey messages on behalf of the mysterious proprietor.

INT. LOBBY. DAY

Zero, substituting at the concierge desk, looks up to a high window across the room where the shadowy figures of M. Gustave and Deputy Kovacs meet in a storage pantry. A clerk with a pot belly flips the pages in a ledger book and takes notes. He is Herr Becker.

35

MR. MOUSTAFA
(*voice-over*)
On these occasions, M. Gustave and our business manager,
Herr Becker, met with him in private consultation
above Reception.

Cut to:

*A plain, graceful, seventeen-year-old beanpole with freckles and a
birthmark the shape of Mexico on the side of her face. She is Agatha.
She works a rolling-pin over a wide expanse of flattened pastry dough.
There are carts circled around her filled with trays of exceptionally
well-made, beautifully decorated pastries shaped like hourglass figures.
(These are Courtesans au chocolat.)*

MR. MOUSTAFA
(*voice-over*)
This was also when I met Agatha –

*Agatha pauses to dry the perspiration on her brow with the back of her
sleeve. She resumes her rolling.*

EXT. BAKERY. DAY

*The timber-frame storefront of a tiny patisserie. A large sign painted
in delicate, pink cursive across the glass reads:* MENDL'S. *There is a
heavy-set baker in an apron with flour over every inch of himself
standing in the doorway. He is Herr Mendl.*

*Agatha rides a rickety bicycle up the alley next to the shop and rings
a bell as she rattles down the cobblestone lane. She bears a milkmaid's
yoke balanced across her shoulders overloaded with sixty small, pink
pastry-boxes tied with string.*

Cut to:

*Agatha gripping the handlebars as she bounces pedaling down the
road.*

MR. MOUSTAFA
(*voice-over*)
– but we won't discuss that.

Title:

PART 2: 'MADAME C.V. D. u.T.'

EXT. TOWN SQUARE. MORNING

Dawn. The platz in the center of Nebelsbad is deserted. Zero emerges briskly from a press kiosk carrying a thick stack of newspapers. He looks down, scanning headlines, as he crosses the street.

Zero stops. His eyes are glued to one of the articles. He skims it. He quickly re-reads it twice more. His mouth falls open.

He bolts off at a sprint.

EXT. FRONT ENTRANCE. MORNING

Zero races up the steps into the hotel carrying the stack of newspapers.

INT. LOBBY. MORNING

Zero dashes past Reception carrying the stack of newspapers.

INT. ROTUNDA. MORNING

Zero mounts the staircase three steps at a time carrying the stack of newspapers.

INT. CORRIDOR. MORNING

Zero speed-walks to the end of the hallway and stops in front of a door labeled PRINCE HEINRICH SUITE. *A sign on the knob reads: 'Do Not Disturb'. Zero hesitates, then knocks. Pause. The door opens a crack and an irritated M. Gustave in a purple, silk dressing gown looks out.*

M. GUSTAVE

What do you want?

ZERO
(*a frantic whisper*)

Look.

Zero holds up the stack of newspapers. M. Gustave picks one off the top and studies it.

Insert:

The front page of the Trans-Alpine Yodel. *The headline is:* WILL THERE BE WAR? TANKS AT FRONTIER – *but a column below the fold reads:*

DOWAGER COUNTESS FOUND DEAD IN BOUDOIR.

A photograph shows Madame D.'s corpse flat on her back on a white carpet.

As M. Gustave reads the article, he says gravely:

> M. GUSTAVE
>
Dear God.

> ZERO
> *(sadly)*
>
I'm terribly sorry, sir.

> M. GUSTAVE
> *(melodramatic but pained)*
>
We must go to her.

> ZERO
> *(hesitates)*
>
We must?

> M. GUSTAVE
>
Tout de suite. She needs me – and I need *you*: to help me with my bags and so on.

An old woman's voice calls from the next room, coquettish:

> FRENCH LADY
> *(out of shot)*
>
Tout va bien, ma chérie?

> M. GUSTAVE
> *(sharply)*
>
Attendez-moi, darling.

> *(to Zero:)*
>
How fast can you pack?

ZERO
(*short pause*)

Five minutes.

M. GUSTAVE

Do it – and bring a bottle of the Pouilly-Jouvet '26 in an ice bucket with two glasses so we don't have to drink the cat-piss they serve in the dining car.

ZERO

Yes, sir.

M. Gustave slams the door, and Zero dashes away down the corridor.

INT. TRAIN COMPARTMENT. DAY

A first-class stateroom on the express to Lutz. The snowy foothills of the Zubrowkian Alps whiz by outside. M. Gustave and Zero each hold a glass of chilled white wine. There are tears in M. Gustave's eyes.

M. GUSTAVE

I blame myself.

M. Gustave checks the color of the wine in the light. It is excellent.

M. GUSTAVE

She tried to tell me she had a premonition. I didn't listen. (*Imagining the scene.*) All of Lutz will be dressed in black – except her own ghastly, deceitful children whom she loathed and couldn't bear to kiss hello. They'll be dancing like gypsies.

Zero nods soberly. M. Gustave becomes philosophical/nihilistic:

There's really no point in doing anything in life, because it's all over in the blink of an eye – and, the next thing you know, *rigor mortis* sets in. Oh, how the good die young! With any luck, she's left a few Klubecks for *your* old friend – (*motioning to himself*) but one never knows until the ink is dry on the death certificate. She was dynamite in the sack, by the way.

ZERO
(*scandalized in spite of himself*)
She was *eighty-four*, M. Gustave!

39

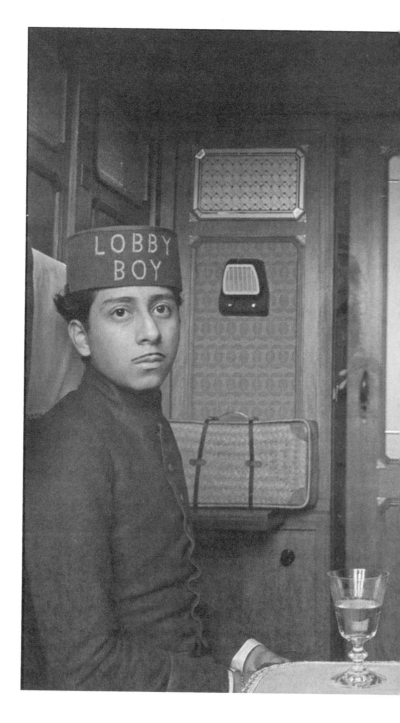

M. GUSTAVE
(*pause*)

I've had older.

M. Gustave throws back the rest of his glass and refills it as he expands on the point:

M. GUSTAVE

When you're young, it's all filet steak, but as the years go by, you have to move onto the cheaper cuts – which is fine with me, because I *like* those. More flavorful, or so they say. (*Shrugs.*) Why are we stopping at a barley field?

The train has, in fact, come to a halt in the middle of nowhere. Noises echo from the other end of the coach: a door slams open; loud voices argue; heavy footsteps approach.

Three soldiers appear in the compartment doorway. They are stocky, thick-necked, and armed with carbine rifles. They wear grey uniforms and long coats. M. Gustave says with an air of 'fancy-meeting-you-here':

M. GUSTAVE

Well, hello there, chaps.

SOLDIER I
(*blankly*)

Documents, please.

M. GUSTAVE

With pleasure.

M. Gustave withdraws his passport from his coat pocket and presents it to the soldier. The soldier begins to flip through it. M. Gustave gestures toward the photograph of himself:

M. GUSTAVE

It's not a very flattering portrait, I'm afraid. I was once considered a great beauty.

The soldier ignores this comment. M. Gustave peers at the breast pocket of his uniform.

Insert:

A name tag pinned below a military badge. It reads: 'Cpl. F. Miller'.

42

M. Gustave raises an eyebrow and asks pointedly:

> M. GUSTAVE
>
> What's the 'F' stand for? Fritz? Franz?

> SOLDIER I
> *(hesitates)*
>
> Franz.

> M. GUSTAVE
> *(exceedingly pleased)*
>
> I knew it!

The soldier returns the passport to M. Gustave and looks to Zero. Zero nervously hands him a creased and tattered little scrap of paper covered with stamps and seals. The soldier frowns and studies it. M. Gustave smiles, uneasy, and says lightly:

> M. GUSTAVE
>
> He's making a funny face. (*To the soldier.*) That's a Migratory Visa with Stage Three Worker Status, Franz, darling. He's with me.

The soldier shows the scrap of paper to his associates. They confer rapidly at a whisper. There is some debate. Finally, the soldier waves for Zero to follow him:

> FIRST SOLDIER
>
> Come outside, please.

Zero swallows hard and begins to rise – but M. Gustave motions sharply for him to stop. He says, a bit stern:

> M. GUSTAVE
>
> Now wait a minute. (*To Zero.*) Sit down, Zero. (*To the soldiers.*) His papers are in order. I cross-referenced them myself with the Bureau of Labor and Servitude. You can't arrest him simply because he's a bloody immigrant. He hasn't done anything wrong.

The soldier hesitates. He turns to his associates again. They look back at him, expressionless. The soldier grabs Zero by the arm and jerks him out of his seat. M. Gustave is instantly on his feet, tussling.

M. GUSTAVE

Stop it! Stop, damn you!

ZERO

(*in disbelief*)

Never mind, M. Gustave! Let them proceed!

M. Gustave is slammed and held against one wall while Zero is pounded into another. M. Gustave shouts and struggles.

M. GUSTAVE

What are you doing? That hurts!

In two seconds: both M. Gustave and Zero are locked in handcuffs with their arms behind their backs. At this point, M. Gustave explodes:

M. GUSTAVE

You filthy, goddamn, pock-marked, fascist assholes! (*In a pure rage.*) Take your hands off my lobby boy!

M. Gustave and Zero lock eyes across the fracas. In an instant: they are brothers. A new voice shouts from the end of the corridor:

HENCKELS

(*out of shot*)

What's the problem?

All the soldiers snap to attention as a young officer appears in the doorway. He is well-groomed and clean-shaven. He wears a dress-grey uniform with a cape. He is Henckels. The first soldier hands him the scrap of paper and starts to explain the situation – but M. Gustave interrupts calmly with blood trickling from his nose:

M. GUSTAVE

This is outrageous. The young man works for me at the Grand Budapest Hotel in Nebelsbad.

Henckels turns suddenly to M. Gustave. He stares. He says in a quiet voice:

HENCKELS

M. Gustave?

M. Gustave looks at Henckels, curious. He nods slowly.

HENCKELS

My name is Henckels. I'm the son of Dr. and Mrs.
Wolfgang Henckels-Bergersdorfer. Do you remember me?

M. GUSTAVE

I know exactly who you are. It's uncanny. You're little Albert.

HENCKELS

I'm terribly embarrassed. (*To the soldiers.*) Release them.

*The soldiers immediately remove the handcuffs from both M. Gustave
and Zero while Henckels takes out a notebook and begins to scribble
something on a yellow ticket. M. Gustave sits down and presses his
pink handkerchief to his nostril. Henckels says as he writes:*

HENCKELS

Your colleague is stateless. He'll need to apply for a revised
Special Transit Permit, which, honestly, at this point, may
be very difficult to acquire. Take this.

*Henckels finishes writing, tears the ticket out of his notebook, and
hands it to M. Gustave.*

HENCKELS

It's temporary, but it's the best I can offer, I'm afraid.

M. GUSTAVE

How's your wonderful mother?

HENCKELS

Very well, thank you.

M. GUSTAVE

I adore her. Send my love.

HENCKELS

I will.

*Henckels motions politely for Zero to return to his seat and hands the
scrap of paper back to him. Zero tucks it carefully into an envelope.
His hands are shaking. Henckels says gently:*

Your companion was very kind to me when I was a lonely
little boy. (*To both M. Gustave and Zero.*) My men and I
apologize for disturbing you.

Henckels turns coldly to the first soldier. He looks sheepish. He says, robotic, to M. Gustave:

SOLDIER I

I beg your pardon, sir.

Henckels and the soldiers immediately leave the compartment, march down the corridor, and exit the coach. Silence.

M. GUSTAVE

You see? There *are* still faint glimmers of civilization left in this barbaric slaughterhouse that was once known as humanity. Indeed, that's what *we* provide in our own modest, humble, insignificant – (*Sighs deeply.*) Oh, fuck it.

M. Gustave looks out the window as the train begins to move again. Zero appears to be in a state of numb shock.

Montage:

The cosmopolitan city of Lutz in the dead of night. A rickety Daimler taxi sputters along a winding cobblestone road at top speed. It squeezes up a narrow lane lined with shops. All are closed and shuttered. It dips into a tunnel through a brick building. It crosses a stone bridge high over a river. It drives through an iron gate, circles around a garden, and skids to a stop next to Madame D.'s limousine.

Up a short path, there is an enormous mansion.

INT. FOYER. DAY

A bell rings. Feet clack and echo on the wide marble floor. A maid in black hurries to open the front door. She is Clotilde. M. Gustave and Zero enter the vestibule while the taxi waits outside. M. Gustave kisses Clotilde on both cheeks and says immediately:

M. GUSTAVE

Where is she, Clotilde? Take me to her.

Clotilde leads M. Gustave with Zero in tow through a series of doors, enfilade, until they arrive at a dimly candlelit drawing room.

Murals of cherubs cover the walls. There is a harpsichord in one corner and a loudly ticking grandfather clock in another. The feet of the corpse,

46

in silver pumps, jut out, toes up, from inside the casket on top of a gold-leaf table.

M. Gustave stops and gasps. He turns to Clotilde and nods. She tugs Zero by the sleeve, and they withdraw. M. Gustave picks up a chair, carries it to the body, sets it down, and sits. Silence. He speaks in a normal, conversational voice:

M. GUSTAVE

You're looking *so* well, darling. You really are. They've done a marvelous job. I don't know what sort of cream they've put on you down at the morgue, but I *want* some. Honestly, you look better than you have in years. You look like you're alive!

M. Gustave shakes his head in admiration. He leans down and kisses Madame D. on the lips. Zero and Clotilde, watching discreetly from the shadows in the next room, look slightly revolted.

M. Gustave takes the corpse's hand. He notices something and hesitates.

Insert:

Madame D.'s fingernails. They are now lacquered in a rich plum. M. Gustave says, deeply moved:

M. GUSTAVE

You changed it, after all. It's perfect. (*Calling to the next room.*) Clotilde?

Clotilde advances into view. She says respectfully:

MAID

Oui, M. Gustave?

M. GUSTAVE

A glass of chilled water with no ice, please.

CLOTIDE

Oui, M. Gustave – et aussi: M. Serge a demandé un mot avec vous en privé dans son office, s'il vous plaît.

M. GUSTAVE
(*slightly irritated*)

Oh. Well, all right. (*Distracted, to the body.*) I shan't be long, darling.

M. Gustave stands up and follows Clotilde through the row of doors. Zero looks back at the casket as he trails behind them.

>   MR. MOUSTAFA
>   (*voice-over*)
> We were escorted through a green baize door, down a
> narrow service corridor, and into the butler's pantry.

INT. OFFICE. NIGHT

A small chamber separated from the kitchen by a glass-paneled wall. M. Gustave checks his watch. There is a cup of water in his hand. Zero drinks a sip of milk. In the background, a sous-chef chops while the cook stirs a bubbling broth. Kitchen and scullery maids dart back and forth clanking pots and pans.

>   MR. MOUSTAFA
>   (*voice-over*)
> A moment later, the kitchen passage swung open, and a
> small servant dressed in white jolted into the room.

An extremely anxious, petite butler enters with an ice bucket. He is Serge. He hacks chips off a frozen block in the sink and fills the container briskly. He turns to go – then spots M. Gustave looking out at him from inside the pantry.

>   MR. MOUSTAFA
>   (*voice-over*)
> I've never forgotten the look on that man's face.

Serge is: deeply distraught, physically exhausted, and, above all, terrified. He swallows, holds up a quick finger for M. Gustave to wait, then disappears back out the door. M. Gustave frowns. He says to himself:

>   M. GUSTAVE
> What the devil is going on?

M. Gustave looks to Zero. Zero is perplexed.

>   MR. MOUSTAFA
>   (*voice-over*)
> I, myself, had never set foot inside a house of this kind in
> my life.

M. Gustave dumps his glass of water into a potted cactus and strides through the chaotic kitchen while Clotilde watches him with a feather duster in her hand. She makes a reluctant move to advise him to stop – but he flies past her, bangs out the swinging door after Serge, and marches into a dark corridor.

> MR. MOUSTAFA
> (*voice-over*)

I understood very little about the events that were to follow – but, eventually, I came to recognize:

INT. TROPHY ROOM. NIGHT

A door opens. M. Gustave comes inside and stops short. He hesitates. Zero sidles in next to him. They both stare, mouths open.

> MR. MOUSTAFA
> (*voice-over*)

When the destiny of a great fortune is at stake, men's greed spreads like a poison in the bloodstream.

Cut to:

A dark, woody parlor with mounted heads everywhere – lions, tigers, buffaloes, antelopes, etc. A murmuring audience of fifty men in business suits is gathering and taking its seats in rows before a dais. Every age, build, and variety of facial hair is accounted for. Some carry briefcases and canes. Most have strong drinks in their hands. There are also several young dandies; a few little old ladies; and a pair of country farmers.

> MR. MOUSTAFA
> (*voice-over*)

Uncles, nephews, cousins – in-laws of increasingly tenuous connection. The old woman's most distant relations had come foraging out of the woodwork.

Serge drops an ice cube into a glass of whiskey with tongs. He does a double-take as he sees that M. Gustave has followed him into the room.

> MR. MOUSTAFA
> (*voice-over*)

At the head of this congregation (it was a disorienting coincidence), we discovered our own Deputy Kovacs

49

(himself an important attorney, of course). He was the executor of the dead widow's estate.

Deputy Kovacs, standing behind a desk on a platform at the front of the room, squints at M. Gustave, puzzled. M. Gustave and Zero look back at him, equally confused. Deputy Kovacs turns his attention back to the seated audience. He clears his throat, sets a large, cardboard box down in front of him, and addresses the room:

DEPUTY KOVACS

This is Madame D.'s Last Will and Testament. It consists of a general tontine drawn up before the event of her husband's death forty-six years ago –

Deputy Kovacs lifts a faded, fragile slip of paper out of the box. He places it delicately on the table.

– in combination with 635 amendments, notations, corrections, and letters of wishes executed during the subsequent decades.

Deputy Kovacs reaches into the box with two hands and pulls out an enormous pile of scraps, slips, shreds, slivers, forms, files, postcards, and various bits of lint and loose thread. He plants it all down with a thud.

The ultimate legality of this accumulation requires further analysis; but, in the opinion of this office, it was Madame D.'s intention that control of the vast bulk of her estate should be transferred, forthwith, to her son, Dmitri –

Cut to:

A spindly, thirty-five-year-old man with a thick head of spiky, black hair which sticks up straight into the air. He has black eyes and a black moustache. He wears a black suit cut close to his skinny body. He is Dmitri. A thug in a leather coat with close-shaven head and high-heeled boots sits slightly behind and beside him. He wears brass knuckles on both hands. He is Jopling.

– with special allowances for his sisters Marguerite, Laetizia, and Carolina –

Cut to:

Madame D.'s spinster daughters. They range in age from forty to fifty.
They are sturdy and fierce.

> – and minor gifts for various members of the extended
> family as shown in the List of Recipients, which I will
> elucidate in due course.

There is a mumbling of general approval around the room and
throughout the gallery of distant relations. A few take notes. Deputy
Kovacs interjects:

> However.

Voices hush. Pause.

> An additional codicil, delivered into my possession by post
> only this morning, and, by all indications, sent by Madame
> D. during the last hours of her life, contains an amendment
> to the original certificate, which, as prescribed by law, I will
> read to you now. The authenticity of this document has not
> yet been confirmed by the presiding magistrate, so I ask
> that all parties be patient and refrain from comment until
> such time as our investigations can be completed.

Dmitri and Jopling confer in a tense whisper. The sisters grumble,
dismayed. The group as a whole sits up to attention. Deputy Kovacs
slides a handwritten letter on pale-pink paper out of an envelope and
reads:

DEPUTY KOVACS

> 'To my esteemed friend who comforted me in my later
> years and brought sunshine into the life of an old woman
> who thought she would never be happy again – M. Gustave
> H. – I bequeath, bestow, and devise, free of all taxation and
> with full and absolute fiduciary entitlement, the painting
> known as "Boy with Apple" –'

M. GUSTAVE
(*floored*)

Wow!

DEPUTY KOVACS

> '– by Johannes van Hoytl –'

M. Gustave grips Zero by the shoulder like a vise. Zero grimaces.

M. GUSTAVE

I can't believe it.

DEPUTY KOVACS

'– the younger –'

Dmitri drops a tumbler on the floor. He blurts angrily:

DMITRI

What?

DEPUTY KOVACS

'– which gave us both so much pleasure.'

Deputy Kovacs looks up. The three sisters talk loudly over each other simultaneously:

MARGEURITE

The van Hoytl?

LAETIZIA

Tax-free?

CAROLINA

Can she do that?

A hunched, ancient, grizzled, old man in the middle of the room throws up his hands. He asks loudly:

OLD MAN

Who's Gustave H.?

M. GUSTAVE
(*inevitably*)

I'm afraid that's me, darling.

Every face in the entire assembly now turns around fully and stares at M. Gustave and Zero. Silence.

The room erupts. All the distant relations start talking at once. Dmitri is on his feet, advancing toward the back of the room, flanked by Jopling, as he explodes, pointing at M. Gustave.

DMITRI

That fucking faggot! He's a concierge. What are you doing here?

M. GUSTAVE
(*stiffening*)
I've come to pay my respects to a great woman whom I loved.

DMITRI
(*turning to the room*)
This man is an intruder in my home!

M. GUSTAVE
(*making a point of it*)
It's not yours *yet*, Dmitri. Only when probate is granted, and the Deed of Entitlement –

DMITRI

You're not getting 'Boy with Apple', you goddamn little fruit!

M. GUSTAVE
(*genuinely offended*)
How's that supposed to make me feel?

The three sisters join Dmitri as the veins in his neck begin to bulge. He continues loudly, for the record:

DMITRI

Call the police. We're pressing charges. This criminal has plagued my family for nearly twenty years. He's a ruthless adventurer and a con artist who preys on mentally feeble, sick old ladies – and he probably fucks them, too!

The three sisters look horrified. One of the little old ladies gasps. Shocked faces look to M. Gustave. He shrugs and says tentatively:

M. GUSTAVE
I go to bed with all my friends.

Dmitri cold-cocks M. Gustave an upper-cut to the jaw and drops him with one punch. Less than a second later, Zero slams his own fist squarely right into the middle of Dmitri's face and knocks him over backward with blood spurting out of his nose. Less than a second after that, Jopling pounds Zero in the side of the head, sending him flying with a smack against the wall and melting instantly into the floor. The room breaks into complete pandemonium.

In the midst of the chaos, the hunched old man says, aside, to a younger one:

OLD MAN

Where's Céline?

YOUNG MAN
(*hesitates*)

She's *dead*. We're reading her will.

OLD MAN
(*slightly embarrassed*)

Oh, quite right, of course. How silly of me.

Another younger man, eavesdropping, starts coughing and spits red wine into his glass.

In the meantime: Serge helps M. Gustave and Zero to their feet as Jopling restrains Dmitri, and various of the distant relations attempt to intervene in the fray. Dmitri, behind an almost certainly broken nose, shouts furiously at M. Gustave as he strains to clamber over his henchman's shoulder:

DMITRI

If I learn you ever once laid a finger on my mother's body, living or dead, I swear to God, I'll cut your throat! (*Screaming.*) You hear me?

M. GUSTAVE
(*clever though dizzy*)

I thought I was supposed to be a fucking faggot.

DMITRI
(*hesitates*)

You are, but you're bisexual!

M. GUSTAVE
(*pause*)

Let's change the subject. I'm leaving.

M. Gustave turns and, assisted by Serge and a staggering Zero, exits the room.

INT. KITCHEN. NIGHT

Clotilde rushes to M. Gustave's assistance as Serge brings him through the door. She brushes his shoulders and smooths his hair. Serge shouts frantically in French and guides them all back into his butler's pantry. Zero holds his glass of milk against his ear like an ice-pack. Serge and Clotilde yell at each other while the other servants race in and out of the kitchen, panicking. They disappear again into the next room.

M. Gustave and Zero, alone for a moment, catch their breath.
M. Gustave pants:

> M. GUSTAVE
> That picture – 'Boy with Apple' – is priceless. Understand?

> ZERO
> *(hopeful)*
> Congratulations, M. Gustave!

> M. GUSTAVE
> They're going to fight me for the son of a bitch.

> ZERO
> Is it very beautiful?

> M. GUSTAVE
> *(swooning)*
> Beyond description. (*Reciting.*) 'E'en the most gifted bard's rhyme can only sing but to the *lack* of her and all she *isn't*! His tongue doth trip –'

> ZERO
> Can I see it?

M. Gustave looks surprised. Pause.

> M. GUSTAVE
> I don't see why not.

M. Gustave zooms out through the scullery and into a little stairwell. Zero follows. They spiral up a steep flight.

Cut to:

A wide landing overlooking the foyer. The voices of the bickering assembly echo from the rear of the house. M. Gustave looks quickly left and right, then darts down the hallway and through a set of double doors.

INT. LIBRARY. NIGHT

A long, narrow gallery lined from floor to ceiling with books and paintings. M. Gustave leads Zero straight through to the far end where 'Boy with Apple' hangs above a fireplace. He stands beside it facing Zero and assumes the role of a museum docent:

> M. GUSTAVE
> This is van Hoytl's exquisite portrayal of a beautiful boy on the cusp of manhood. Blond, smooth. Skin as white as *that* milk. (*Pointing to Zero's glass.*) Of impeccable provenance. One of the last in private hands – and, unquestionably, the best. It's a masterpiece. The rest of this shit is worthless junk.

M. Gustave and Zero stand side by side and admire the picture for a long minute – then Zero looks strangely to M. Gustave. M. Gustave looks back at him, curious. Zero's eyes flicker. M. Gustave frowns.

Zero goes to the corner, picks up a footstool, and places it on the hearth.

M. Gustave hesitates. He steps up onto the footstool. He lifts the painting off its hooks. He comes back down to the floor. There is a dark rectangle in the wallpaper marking the absent picture. He turns to Zero again, uncertain.

Behind the fire-irons, leaning against a stack of etchings, Zero spots a woodcut print of two lesbians masturbating. He grabs it and hangs it in the painting's place.

INT. FOYER. NIGHT

M. Gustave and Zero circle rapidly down the wide staircase. Serge comes into the room at the same time and meets them as they arrive at the front door. He says breathlessly:

SERGE

M. Gustave! *Pardonnez-moi. Ce n'est pas –*

Serge sees the painting tucked under M. Gustave's arm. He stares at it. He says reluctantly:

SERGE

Je peux vous aider?

M. GUSTAVE

Oui, Serge. Vous pouvez emballer celui-là.

SERGE
(*hesitates*)

Emballer – 'Boy with Apple'?

M. Gustave nods and hands Serge the picture. Serge takes it. Pause. He goes over to a bureau, withdraws a large sheet of wrapping-paper, folds it around the painting, and ties it with string. He returns the parcel to M. Gustave.

M. GUSTAVE

Merci, Serge.

Serge opens the front door. M. Gustave and Zero quickly go outside and get into the taxi. Serge, overwhelmed and confused, with tears in his eyes, looks in at them through one of the back-seat windows. M. Gustave rolls it down.

M. GUSTAVE

What'd you want to tell me? Before.

SERGE
(*long pause, with a heavy accent*)

I think I cannot say right now.

M. GUSTAVE
(*short pause*)

Write me tomorrow. (*Sharply, to the driver.*) Lutzbahn Station!

The taxi's tires squeal, and the car shoots down the driveway. Serge watches, deeply anguished and disturbed.

INT. TRAIN COMPARTMENT. NIGHT

A sleeper on the overnight to Nebelsbad. The bunks have been folded down and made up, and both M. Gustave and Zero wear pajamas. (M. Gustave's are of burgundy silk and belted.)

'Boy with Apple', partially unwrapped, is on display, balanced along the edge of the washbasin. M. Gustave says soberly:

> M. GUSTAVE
>
> I'll never part with it. It reminded her of me. It will remind me of her. Always. I'll die with this picture above my bed. (*Quickly.*) See the resemblance?

M. Gustave positions himself alongside the painting. Zero mutters politely from his bed:

> ZERO
>
> Oh, yes.

M. Gustave lies down. He stares up at the ceiling. Pause.

> M. GUSTAVE
>
> Actually, we should sell it. Sooner rather than later, in case they try and steal it back. Plus: something about those lunatic foot-soldiers on the express – I think this could be a tricky war and a long dry spell in the hotel trade. For all we know, they could board us up tomorrow.

Zero looks alarmed. M. Gustave sits up again and signals for him to come closer. Zero joins him.

> M. GUSTAVE
>
> Let's make a solemn blood-pact. We'll contact the black-market and liquidate 'Boy with Apple' by the end of the week, then leave the country and lay low somewhere along the Maltese Riviera until the troubles blow over and we resume our posts. In exchange for your help, your loyalty, and your services as my personal valet, I pledge to you: one-point-five percent of the net sale price.

Zero takes this in. He says quietly:

ZERO
One-point-five.

                    M. GUSTAVE
Plus room and board.

                    ZERO
                 (*optimistic*)
Could we make it ten?

                    M. GUSTAVE
                 (*in disbelief*)
Ten? Are you joking? That's more than I'd pay an actual
dealer – and you wouldn't know chiaroscuro from chicken
giblets. No, one-point-five is correct – but I'll tell you what:
if I die first, and I most certainly will, *you* will be my sole
heir. There's not much in the kitty except a set of ivory-
backed hairbrushes and my library of romantic poetry –
but, when the time comes, these will be yours, along with
whatever we haven't already spent on whores and whiskey.
This is our sacred bond. I'll draw it up right now.

*Pause. Zero nods. M. Gustave whisks a drinks menu out of a slot on
the wall, places it face down on the night-stand, and sets a fountain
pen on top of it. He dictates:*

                    M. GUSTAVE
I, M. Gustave H., being of relatively sound mind and body,
on this day the twenty-seventh of October in the year of our
Lord nineteen hundred and –

Zero quickly uncaps the pen and begins to write.

INT. STORAGE PANTRY. DAY

*The next morning. A vault adjacent to the meeting room above the
lobby. There are rows of safety-deposit boxes with engraved room
numbers along the walls. M. Gustave hides the wrapped package
behind a radiator. He takes a fur stole off a coat-hanger and drapes it
awkwardly over the top. They exit the room. M. Gustave closes the
heavy, inner door and spins the combination lock, then slides an outer
one shut and bolts it with a key.*

ANATOLE
(*out of shot*)

Excuse me.

M. Gustave and Zero jump. They turn around quickly and see Anatole standing in the doorway. M. Gustave mumbles, anxious:

M. GUSTAVE

Uh-huh?

ANATOLE
(*intrigued*)

The police are here. They asked for you.

Silence. M. Gustave nods. He says cheerily:

M. GUSTAVE

Tell them we'll be right down.

Anatole goes back down the steps. M. Gustave and Zero look down into the lobby through a window. Eight uniformed officers wait at the concierge desk. M. Gustave says tensely:

61

M. GUSTAVE

Have you ever been questioned by the authorities?

ZERO
(*grimly*)

Yes, on one occasion, I was arrested and tortured by the rebel militia after the Desert Uprising.

M. GUSTAVE
(*hesitates*)

Right. Well, you know the drill, then. Zip it.

ZERO

Of course.

M. GUSTAVE

You've never heard the word 'van Hoytl' in your life.

ZERO

Got it.

M. GUSTAVE

OK. Let's go.

M. Gustave and Zero descend into the lobby. M. Gustave's face brightens as he crosses the room and greets the visitors:

M. GUSTAVE

How may we serve you, gentlemen?

POLICE CAPTAIN
(*producing a warrant*)

By order of the Commissioner of Police, Zubrowka Province, I hereby place you under arrest for the murder of Madame Céline Villeneuve Desgoffe und Taxis.

M. GUSTAVE
(*somehow vindicated*)

I *knew* there was something fishy! We never got the cause of *death*! She's been *murdered* – and you think *I* did it.

M. Gustave turns away and breaks into a sprint through the lobby. The police chase him. Zero watches, stunned.

Title:

PART 3: CHECKPOINT 19
CRIMINAL INTERNMENT CAMP

EXT. PRISON. DAY

A buttressed castle on a high rock spur. Clusters of tangled barbed-wire decorate the tops of the walls above a sheer cliff that drops straight down into the medieval village below.

Zero stands waiting with a small pink pastry-box in his hands. There is a guard with a tommy gun next to him. Silence.

A hidden gear begins to crank, and a heavy iron and oak gate swings slowly open. The guard makes an offhand toss of the head to signal for Zero to proceed. Zero nods politely and starts across a narrow bridge over a moat. Two more guards wait at the far end in front of the doors to a fortified keep.

INT. VISITING ROOM. DAY

A converted armory containing a row of chairs along an extended table with a penitentiary-style wire-glass partition down the middle. Zero sits alone. The pastry-box is in front of him next to a glass of water. A door opens, and another guard escorts M. Gustave into the room.

M. Gustave is now dressed in a striped prison uniform with his cap worn at a slight tilt. His hands are shackled. His face is purple and misshapen, covered almost entirely with bruises and abrasions, with one eye swollen completely shut. He sits down facing Zero on the other side of the partition. (There is a glass of water for him, as well.)

The guard waits in the corner. He checks his watch.

Zero looks horrified. He gasps:

                    ZERO
What happened?

                    M. GUSTAVE
What happened, my dear Zero, is I beat the living shit out
of a snivelling little runt called Pinky Bandinski who had

63

the gall to question my virility – because if there's one thing we've learned from penny dreadfuls, it's that, when you find yourself in a place like this, you must never be a candy-ass. You've got to prove yourself from day one. You've got to win their respect. Of course, I've got about a foot and a half of reach on Pinky, so once I'd pried him loose out from under my armpit, it was short order before I whipped him into scrambled eggs. (*Takes a sip of water.*) You should take a long look at *his* ugly mug this morning. (*Spits blood back into the cup.*) He's actually become a dear friend. You'll meet him, I hope. So.

M. Gustave slides closer to the glass. So does Zero.

You talk to Kovacs?

> ZERO
> I saw him last night in secret. He made me take an oath (on a Bible). I wouldn't tell a soul. You're supposed to, also.

> M. GUSTAVE
> (*irritated*)
> I'll do that later.

> ZERO
> He suspects you're innocent.

> M. GUSTAVE
> Of course he does. What's the charge?

INT. TAVERN. NIGHT

An alcove in a corner of a dark, seedy, back-street alehouse. Shady characters lurk at the counter. Zero sits across from Deputy Kovacs, who reads a report to him by the light of an oil-lamp. They both sip mugs of lager. There is also a small Bible on the table.

> DEPUTY KOVACS
> 'In the small hours of the evening of nineteen October, an individual well-known to the house and staff, a M. Gustave H., did arrive at the Desgoffe und Taxis residence in Lutz and enter by the rear service alley, alerting no one to his

presence, and did then proceed by way of back-stairs and servants' passage to deliver himself into the private chambers of Madame D. There is no evidence to indicate whether this visit had been prearranged with her or not. The next morning, Madame D. was found dead by strychnine poisoning. M. Gustave was not observed on the premises again until –' of course – 'twenty-four hours later.' The identity of his accusers is made clear in this notarized deposition.

Deputy Kovacs produces another document which he hands to Zero. Zero studies it as Deputy Kovacs continues:

DEPUTY KOVACS
They include, essentially, all members of the extended family – but the key witness who actually (ostensibly) saw the alleged events appears to have fled the jurisdiction. His whereabouts are currently unknown, but he's being sought and pursued by the relevant authorities.

ZERO
(*concerned*)
Who *is* he?

Cut to:

M. Gustave with a look of utter astonishment on his face. He blurts out:

M. GUSTAVE
Serge?

ZERO
I'm afraid so.

M. GUSTAVE
That little *prick.*

Pause. M. Gustave reconsiders.

M. GUSTAVE
No, I don't believe it. They put him up to it. I've been dropped into a nest of vipers.

ZERO
You have an alibi?

M. GUSTAVE
(*offhand*)

Certainly, but she's married to the Duke of Westphalia. I can't allow her name to get mixed up in all this monkey business.

ZERO
(*gravely*)

M. Gustave: your *life* may be at stake.

M. GUSTAVE
(*bitterly*)

I know, but the bitch legged it. She's already on the *Queen Nasstasja* halfway to Dutch Tanganyika.

M. Gustave sighs and stares at the floor, shaking his head. He looks like he is about to cry. Zero says finally – almost inaudibly:

ZERO

Don't give up.

M. Gustave looks back to Zero. He nods. He points.

M. GUSTAVE

What's in the box?

ZERO
(*encouraging*)

A Courtesan *au chocolat*.

M. GUSTAVE
(*deeply moved*)

From Mendl's. Thank you, my angel.

EXT. STREET. NIGHT

A dark lane crowded with narrow, crooked little buildings. Rushing water gurgles down the gutters. A pack of rats darts across the road in single-file and disappears into a drainpipe. A church bell rings across the city.

Jopling waits on the threshold of a ramshackle cottage staring at the front door.

MR. MOUSTAFA
(*voice-over*)
The details of the conspiracy, now a matter of public
record, were, at that time, impossible for us to apprehend.

*The door cracks open. A young Washerwoman with a club-foot and a
rag in her hands peers out. Jopling hands the woman his card. She
studies it.*

Insert:

An engraved calling card on bright, white stock which reads:

J. G. Jopling, Esq.
PRIVATE INQUIRY AGENT

The woman looks back up to Jopling, nervous. He says in a low voice:

JOPLING
I'm looking for Serge X. – a young man in the service of my
employers, the family Desgoffe und Taxis of Schloss Lutz.

WASHERWOMAN
(*timidly*)
Yes, sir?

JOPLING
You're his sister?

WASHERWOMAN
Yes, sir.

JOPLING
Seen him lately?

WASHERWOMAN
(*surprised*)
No, sir.

JOPLING
(*doubtful*)
No, sir?

WASHERWOMAN
(*innocent*)
No, sir.

I need to find him right away. For his own safety – (*Pointing in her face.*) And everyone else's. If he shows up?

WASHERWOMAN
(*tentatively*)

Yes, sir?

JOPLING
(*darkly*)

Tell him Jopling says, 'Come home.'

Pause. The woman nods. Jopling turns away and walks over to a black motorcycle parked at the corner.

MR. MOUSTAFA
(*voice-over*)

But one thing was certain: the Desgoffe und Taxis were a very powerful family –

Jopling puts on a pair of goggles, kick-starts his engine, revs the motor, and rumbles away. The woman shuts the door and locks the bolt.

Cut to:

Jopling racing his howling motorcycle through the center of the city at midnight. Under the goggles, his eyes are calm.

MR. MOUSTAFA
(*voice-over*)

– and time was not on our side.

INT. MESS HALL. NIGHT

Another evening meal. The full assembled staff sits at the long table, anxious and curious, murmuring. The cook waits, uncertain, gripping a cauldron by his oven-mitts. A door swings open.

Mr. Mosher and Zero stride into the room. Mr. Mosher holds up an envelope and beckons to Zero.

MR. MOSHER

A letter from M. Gustave. Zero?

The staff whispers excitedly then falls silent as Zero ascends M. Gustave's podium, opens the envelope, and takes out a piece of paper. Pause. Zero clears his throat and reads in a formal voice:

'My dear and trusted colleagues –'

Cut to:

M. Gustave in his cell (where his podium seems to have been magically transported). A gentle halo of light glows behind him. He addresses the camera as he begins his usual pacing:

M. GUSTAVE
– I miss you deeply as I write from the confines of my regrettable and preposterous incarceration. Until I walk amongst you again as a free man, the Grand Budapest remains in your hands – as does its impeccable reputation. Keep it spotless and glorify it. Take extra special care of every little-bitty bit of it as if I were watching over you like a hawk with a horsewhip in its talons – (*brandishing a soup-ladle*) because I *am*. Should I discover a lapse of any variety during my absence, I promise: swift and merciless justice

will descend upon you. A great and noble house has been placed under your protection. (Tell Zero if you see any funny business.)

Cut to:

Zero at podium. He concludes:

> ZERO
>
> 'Your devoted M. Gustave.' Then there's a poem, but we might want to go ahead and start on the soup, since it's forty-six stanzas.

Mr. Mosher signals to the cook. He begins to serve as Zero reads on:

> ZERO
>
> 'A moist, black ash dampens the filth of a dung-dark rat's-nest and mingles with the thick scent of wood-rot while the lark-song of a guttersnipe echoes across a —'

INT. CORRIDOR. DAY

M. Gustave pushes a metal cart with a stack of plates and a steel tureen on it through a barred door. He stops in front of a large cell where four convicts loiter on their bunks playing cards, scratching graffiti on the walls, and looking at dirty pictures.

> M. GUSTAVE
>
> May I offer any of you inmates a plate of mush?

The convicts all look to M. Gustave at once. No one speaks. M. Gustave hesitates.

> No? Anyone? You — with the very large scar on your face?

M. Gustave points to a seven-foot giant with a deep slash from the top corner of his forehead all the way down and across to the other side of his chin. The giant frowns. He stands up. The other convicts look uneasy.

> Come now. Try it. It's, actually, quite warm and nourishing this morning. It needs a dash of salt.

M. Gustave prepares a plate of lumpy gruel for the giant. He shakes in a touch of salt from a shaker. The giant tastes it. Pause. He shrugs, pleased. He nods. M. Gustave smiles.

Good day.

M. Gustave pushes his cart to the next cell. A bald wrestler lifts weights while an old man spots him.

Mush, gents? Any takers?

The wrestler and the old man look at M. Gustave blankly with the bar-bell in the air. M. Gustave shrugs and says regretfully:

Suit yourselves.

M. Gustave pushes his cart to the next cell. These convicts are all asleep. M. Gustave says with a musical lilt:

Rise and shine. Chop-chop!

A wiry, pint-sized convict the shape of a fire hydrant squints out from under his covers. He is Pinky.

Good morning, Pinky.

Pinky yawns and sets his feet to the floor. The convicts in the other bunks also begin to rustle. Their faces are brutal, and their bodies are hard and powerful. They are Günther and Wolf. (A fourth convict, also in the room, begins to get out of bed, as well – but his face is not revealed for the moment.)

M. Gustave reaches to the lower shelf of the cart and produces a pink pastry-box. All the convicts quickly gather at a small table. (The fourth convict sits with his back to the camera.)

Pinky says eagerly:

PINKY

Mendl's again?

M. GUSTAVE

Precisely. Who's got the throat-slitter?

Günther digs in his sock and takes out a small weapon consisting of a half-toothbrush fixed with wire to a hand-slivered straight razor cut into serrated teeth. M. Gustave folds open the pastry-box and cuts a Courtesan au chocolat into careful segments. The convicts eat daintily. Wolf says, chewing:

71

                              WOLF
     Out of this world.

                          M. GUSTAVE
                           (*obviously*)
     Mendl's is the best. Well, back to work.

M. Gustave rises. Pinky says suddenly:

                            PINKY
     Mr. Gustave?

                          M. GUSTAVE
                           (*hesitates*)
     Yeah?

*Pinky exchanges a look with the others. They nod. He darts to the door,
looks up and down the corridor, then closes it softly. He signals for
M. Gustave to sit back down. M. Gustave, slightly puzzled, obeys. They
all lean in closer as Pinky whispers:*

                            PINKY
     Me and the boys talked it over. We think you're a real
     straight fella.

                          M. GUSTAVE
     Well, I've never been accused of that before, but I appreciate
     the sentiment.

                            PINKY
     You're one of us now.

                          M. GUSTAVE
                        (*somewhat moved*)
     What a lovely thing to say. Thank you, dear Pinky. Thank
     you, Günther. Thank you, Wolf. I couldn't ask for a finer
     tribute.

M. Gustave bows slightly. He hesitates.

                          M. GUSTAVE
     Anything else?

Pinky looks to the fourth convict. He nods:

Tell him, Ludwig.

Cut to:

The fourth convict. Numerous short scars chop skinny, bald lines into his shorn scalp. His arms are tattooed heavily with skulls, skeletons, and images of the grim reaper. He has one silver tooth and a bit of butter-cream icing on the side of his mouth. He is Ludwig.

Ludwig takes a deep breath. He launches into his spiel:

LUDWIG

Checkpoint Nineteen ain't no two-bit hoosegow. You got broad-gauge iron bars on every door, vent, and window. You got barb' wire on every containment wall and barricade. You got seventy-two guards on the floor and sixteen more in the towers. You got a 325-foot drop into a moat full of crocodiles – but, like the best of 'em, it's got a soft spot, which in this case happens to take the form of a storm-drain sewer system datin' from the time of the original rock fortification way back in the Middle Ages. Now, nobody's sayin' it's a stroll down a tree-lined promenade with a fine lady and a white poodle, but it's got what you'd call 'vulnerability' – and that's our bread and butter. Take a look.

Ludwig produces a crude but highly detailed map and floor-plan of the castle compound drawn with charcoal on a strip of butcher paper. M. Gustave examines it with fixed concentration. He says pointedly:

M. GUSTAVE

Who drew this?

LUDWIG
(*stiffening*)
What do you mean, 'Who drew this?' I did.

M. GUSTAVE
(*impressed*)
Very good. You've got a wonderful line, Ludwig. This shows great artistic promise.

Ludwig smiles slightly, pleased and slightly embarrassed. M. Gustave points on the map:

M. GUSTAVE

Question: how do you intend to penetrate this lowest rudiment? If I interpret the legend correctly, it's twenty-five inches of reinforced granite masonry, is it not? Digging with the throat-slitter, I expect that would take three to six months of continual effort, during which time several of our members will have been violently executed.

LUDWIG

You hit the nail on the head there, Mr. Gustave. We got fake documents, second-hand street clothes, and a rope ladder made out of sticks and bunk-linens – but we need diggin' tools, and that's provin' hard to come by in this flophouse.

M. Gustave nods gravely. The others slump, listless, and sigh. M. Gustave taps rapidly on the table with the jerry-rigged shiv. Suddenly, he sits up straight and frowns. The others watch him, curious – then look where he is looking.

The camera zooms in slowly toward the crinkled wrapper of the Courtesan au chocolat *as the five inmates all stare at it together.*

Cut to:

Mr. Moustafa and the author at their dinner table surrounded by meats, sauces, and vegetables. Mr. Moustafa is immobile.

AUTHOR
(voice-over)

At this point in the story, the old man fell silent and pushed away his saddle of lamb. His eyes went blank as two stones. I could see he was in distress. 'Are you ill, Mr. Moustafa?' I finally asked. 'Oh, dear me, no,' he said. 'It's only that I don't know now to proceed.' He was crying.

Mr. Moustafa smiles sadly with tears streaming down his cheeks. The author looks worried.

MR. MOUSTAFA

You see, I never speak of Agatha, because – even at the
thought of her name – I'm unable to control my emotions.

*Mr. Moustafa dries his eyes with his napkin, but the tears instantly
return. He shrugs.*

MR. MOUSTAFA

Well, I suppose there's no way around it. You see, she saved
us.

Title:

ONE MONTH EARLIER

INT. CINEMA. NIGHT

*A smoky small-town movie palace. On screen, a battle scene is in
progress: tanks explode while an infantry unit charges out of a trench
into a tornado of machine-gun fire. In the middle of the back row, a
love scene is in progress: Zero and Agatha French-kiss in a clutch with
her shirt half-unbuttoned and his fingers wrapped around her clearly
visible, white breast. Her hand is jammed down into his trousers. No
one else in the scattered audience appears to notice them.*

MR. MOUSTAFA
(*voice-over*)

On our third, formal rendezvous, I had asked for her hand
in marriage, and she had agreed. We did not have fifty
Klubecks between the two of us. No one knew, of course;
but, then, who would have cared? We were both completely
on our own in the world – and we were deeply in love.

EXT. TOWN SQUARE. NIGHT

Dusk. The platz *in the center of Nebelsbad. A carnival fair is in full
swing with a spinning carousel set to a Wurlitzer organ, a bustling
gallery of games, and vendors serving beer and sausages. Agatha holds
Zero's arm as they walk through the crowd. He reaches into his
uniform, pulls out a small gift-wrapped package, and thrusts it into
her hands.*

75

                    ZERO
Here.

                    AGATHA
                    (*startled*)
Thank you!

                    ZERO
It's a book.

                    AGATHA
                    (*hesitates*)
I see.

                    ZERO
Romantic Poetry, Volume One. M. Gustave recommended it.
I have a copy of my own, as well. I ruined the surprise, I
suppose.

                    AGATHA
I'll go ahead and open it, anyway.

                    ZERO
OK.

*Agatha carefully unwraps the package, folds up the paper, and puts the
ribbon into her pocket. Zero flips open the book and points at a flyleaf.*

                    ZERO
Read the inscription.

                    AGATHA
                    (*reading*)
'For my dearest, darling, treasured, cherished Agatha,
whom I worship. With respect, adoration, admiration,
kisses, gratitude, best wishes, and love. From Z. to A.'

Agatha looks to Zero with tears in her eyes. He smiles sadly.

                    MR. MOUSTAFA
                    (*voice-over*)
M. Gustave insisted on an immediate and thorough cross-
examination –

INT. STORAGE PANTRY. DAY

M. Gustave sits opposite Agatha at a long table with his hand resting on top of hers as he leans close to her recounting something vividly. They both laugh uproariously. M. Gustave says loudly, aside, to Zero:

> M. GUSTAVE
> She's *so* charming!

Zero broods in the corner. The table is piled with long-stemmed flowers, and a large, cardboard box overflows with more.

> MR. MOUSTAFA
> (*voice-over*)
> – during which he presented Agatha with a porcelain pendant and five dozen individually tissue-wrapped white tulips in a box the size of a child's coffin.

Insert:

A white porcelain crossed-keys pendant hanging from a velvet ribbon around Agatha's thin neck.

Agatha admires her pendant. Zero grumbles:

> ZERO
> It's not right.

> M. GUSTAVE
> (*hesitates*)
> I beg your pardon? (*Conspiratorially to Agatha.*) Why's he sulking?

> ZERO
> She's my girlfriend. You can't just buy her things.

> M. GUSTAVE
> (*in disbelief*)
> I'm only interviewing this vision of loveliness on *your* behalf. (*Conveying pearls of wisdom.*) Never be jealous in this life, Zero. Not even for an instant.

> ZERO
> (*to Agatha, like a lawyer*)
> Is he flirting with you?

AGATHA

Yes.

Zero looks to M. Gustave with satisfaction. M. Gustave shrugs this off with a wave of the hand, then offers a benediction:

M. GUSTAVE

I approve of this union. (*Still flirting.*) Agatha, my beauty? Return to your beloved.

Zero and Agatha stand together quietly on display, happy. She clutches a tulip. M. Gustave nods sagely.

MR. MOUSTAFA
(voice-over)

Soon, we learned –

INT. PATISSERIE. DAY

The white-marble frosting counter in the back room at Mendl's. There are three, unfinished Courtesans au chocolat *in a row with their tops open. Agatha delicately places a little tool into the fillings of each: a slender file, the head of a small hammer, and a half-scale chisel. As she closes them, she begins to apply a complex series of decorative ripples and swirls.*

> MR. MOUSTAFA
> (*voice-over*)
> – Not only was Agatha immensely skilled with a palette knife and a butter-cream flourish: she was also very brave.

Zero, keeping a lookout at the kitchen door, gives an urgent signal. Agatha swiftly covers the pastries with e damp cheese-cloth just as Herr Mendl crosses into the room, throws open a huge brick-oven, and checks on a batch of gâteaux l'Opéra.

INT. SORTING HALL. DAY

A prison guard searches packages on a metal table. He slices a block of cheese into quarters. He chops-up a loaf of bread into sixths. He opens a double-sized pink pastry-box – and pauses. He stares at the three pristine Courtesans au chocolat.

> MR. MOUSTAFA
> (*voice-over*)
> I believe she was born that way.

The guard gingerly closes the box, slides it aside, unscathed, and moves onto the next package.

INT. LAWYER'S OFFICE. DAY

An art-deco office looking out directly onto the clock tower of Lutzbahn Station. Deputy Kovacs sits behind a wide desk. The box containing Madame D.'s will rests beside him. Its contents have been neatly organized into dozens of little stacks and piles.

Dmitri and his three sisters are seated across from Deputy Kovacs in leather armchairs. Jopling stands in the corner stroking a Siamese cat and staring out the window. Curtains sway in the gentle breeze. Deputy Kovacs sounds concerned:

DEPUTY KOVACS

Something's missing. A crucial document, either misplaced or, conceivably, destroyed. I don't know what it contains, I don't know what it represents, I don't know what it *is* – but there are traces and shadows of it everywhere. (*Motioning to the stacks of paper.*) Now, I don't want to alarm you, and I don't expect to see any significant change in the magistrate's ultimate decision *vis-à-vis* your own inheritance; but, especially given the circumstances of the death, as well as the disappearance of the key witness in the murder case (Serge X.), I suggest we immediately bring this matter to the attention of the municipal inspector so there can be absolutely no question of impropriety at any future date. Agreed?

DMITRI
(*simply*)

Not agreed.

DEPUTY KOVACS
(*puzzled*)

Not agreed?

DMITRI
(*with finality*)

Not agreed.

Silence. The three sisters are stoic. Jopling is stony. Dmitri and Deputy Kovacs stare at each other blankly.

DMITRI

Can I ask you a question, Vilmos?

DEPUTY KOVACS

Yes, Dmitri?

DMITRI

Who you working for?

DEPUTY KOVACS

I beg your pardon?

DMITRI

I thought you're supposed to be *our* lawyer.

81

DEPUTY KOVACS
(*hesitates*)
Well, in point of fact, I'm the executor of the estate. In this particular situation – I represent the deceased.

DMITRI
Oh, yeah?

DEPUTY KOVACS
Yeah. A provision for my fees was included in the –

DMITRI
Just wrap it up, and don't make waves. Agreed?

DEPUTY KOVACS
(*long pause*)
I'm an attorney, Dmitri. I'm obligated to proceed according to the rule of law. Not agreed.

Dmitri's eyes peer sideways. He says quietly, menacing:

DMITRI
This stinks, sisters.

Deputy Kovacs looks insulted. Dmitri stands up, walks to the door, and exits. The cat squeals. Jopling follows Dmitri out the door. Deputy Kovacs' mouth falls open. He points, astonished, across the room:

DEPUTY KOVACS
Did he just throw my cat out the window?

The three sisters turn around quickly. They answer simultaneously:

MARGUERITE
I don't think so.

LAETIZIA
Jopling?

CAROLINA
No. Did he?

Deputy Kovacs waits for the punchline – but it does not come. He dashes to the window and looks down at the sidewalk.

Cut to:

82

A pedestrian in a bowler hat far below standing over a sprawled speck on the sidewalk. He looks up.

Insert:

Four small hammers tap rapid-fire at four half-scale chisels, chipping away into a cement pot-hole. They are making good progress.

INT. LUDWIG'S CELL. NIGHT

M. Gustave, Pinky, Günther, and Ludwig work diligently by candle-light under a wooden table. Periodically, Wolf scoops up the powdery debris with a soup ladle and throws it aside.

Ludwig looks up suddenly, alerted. He holds up a finger.

> LUDWIG
>
> Shh!

M. Gustave, Pinky, and Günther stop tapping at once. They listen attentively. Feet creak along the thick, wooden floor outside the cell – and come to a halt directly in front of the door. Silence.

There is a loud but muffled sneeze.

The feet begin to creak again and fade away until they are inaudible. Ludwig signals to the others. They resume their tapping.

INT. GARRET. NIGHT

An attic bedroom the size of a broom closet. The walls and ceiling are bare planks. Thick beams hold the crooked roof in place. A small skylight window is propped open with a pencil. Zero and Agatha are naked under the rough sheets of her narrow bed. They share a plate of little miniature Courtesans au chocolat. Zero whispers:

> ZERO
>
> There's something I haven't told you, Agatha.

A look of dread crosses Agatha's face. She says reluctantly:

> AGATHA
>
> OK.

ZERO

We stole a painting. It's very valuable (maybe five million Klubecks, in fact). I don't know if anyone's even noticed it's missing yet – but if something should happen to me and M. Gustave –

AGATHA
(evenly)

You stole – art?

ZERO
(defensive)

One picture. Anyway: we need to make a plan for your survival. Hide this.

Zero produces a square of tissue-paper the size of a large postage stamp with neat, minuscule handwriting all over it. Agatha squints at it.

ZERO

It's in code, and you might need a magnifying glass to read it, but it tells you exactly where and how to find 'Boy with Apple'. Don't take less than half the retail asking price. Also –

AGATHA

Zero. I'm a *baker*.

ZERO
(correcting her)

You're a *pastry* chef. One of the best in the –

AGATHA

Not a '*fence*' (if that's the term). I don't trade in stolen property.

ZERO
(hesitates)

I said it wrong. She *willed* it to him!

A door bangs open down the hall. In an instant: Zero jumps out of the bed, leaps with both feet at once into his trousers, and shimmies up out of the skylight.

Cut to:

Zero's point-of-view from the roof. The bedroom door creaks open and Herr Mendl looks in at Agatha. She is now calmly reading her volume of romantic poetry. He grunts:

> HERR MENDL

Go to sleep.

> AGATHA

Yes, Herr Mendl.

The door closes. Agatha looks up to Zero. He holds up the sliver of paper. She shakes her head and whispers:

> AGATHA

No.

> ZERO
> (*pause*)

OK, but take it, anyway.

Zero releases the square of tissue-paper. Agatha sits up quickly as it descends, darting and fluttering, and moves her hand around underneath it while she watches trying to estimate where it is going to land.

At the last second, she reaches up and cleanly plucks it out of the air between thumb and finger.

Zero smiles. He runs away, shoeless, past gutters and chimneys, jumping noiselessly from roof to roof, into the night.

INT. OFFICE BUILDING. NIGHT

A bank of elevators in an art-deco lobby. A bell rings, and a pair of doors slides open. Deputy Kovacs emerges and navigates his way through a maze of suds buckets and women on their hands and knees scrubbing the floor. He does not notice:

Jopling sitting in a chair behind a column reading the evening edition of the Trans-Alpine Yodel.

EXT. STREET. NIGHT

The evening sky is bright blue. Crowds hurry in and out of shops and restaurants. Deputy Kovacs crosses the street and stands next to an old lady at a tram stop. He checks his watch. The tram arrives, and the door opens.

Deputy Kovacs assists the old lady, then boards behind her. He takes a seat. He looks out the window. Just as they pull away, he sees Jopling exit the building and climb onto his motorcycle.

Deputy Kovacs frowns.

Jopling kick-starts his engine and follows the tram, close behind, for three blocks. At the next intersection, a policeman blows a whistle, holds up his hand, and makes Jopling wait while a stream of opposing traffic crosses.

The tram rounds a corner and stops. Deputy Kovacs jumps up and ducks out onto the street. He looks left and right. He hurries up a path toward a grand, colossal, domed palace. A sign carved in stone above the door reads: 'Kunstmuseum Lutz'.

As he goes inside, Deputy Kovacs looks back to see Jopling's motorcycle pulling slowly to the curb.

INT. MUSEUM. NIGHT

The spacious, soaring entrance hall is dim and deserted. One guard sits alone in a corner writing in a logbook. Deputy Kovacs strides across the room. His clacking feet echo broadly. He detours into an antechamber filled with French still-lives. He pauses.

A second set of footsteps clacks through the lobby behind him.

Deputy Kovacs advances rapidly into the next gallery, past a long mural of an ancient war, and descends a staircase. He pauses again at the bottom.

The second set of footsteps continues through the antechamber behind him.

Deputy Kovacs turns a corner and rushes between rows of Greek and Roman statues. He cuts through an Egyptian tomb. He skims through an alcove of iron weapons and suits of armor. He pauses once more and listens.

Silence.

Insert:

A pair of high-heeled boots. Two feet quietly slip out of them and tiptoe away.

Cut to:

Deputy Kovacs looking all around, frantic. Across the room, he sees:

A door labeled VERBOTEN.

Deputy Kovacs runs to the door and opens it. He scans the hall behind him. He sneaks inside.

INT. STORAGE ROOM. NIGHT

Deputy Kovacs flicks on a light. He is in a long hallway lined with racks filled with hundreds of canvases. The room goes dark at either end. He chooses a direction, then sprints straight through into the blackness. Up ahead, he sees lines of faint light around the edges of a door. He skids to a stop and searches for the knob. He turns it and pulls. It is locked. He fumbles at a latch. He snaps it sideways. He swings open the door. His eyes light up:

There is a bicycle leaning against the wall across the alley behind the museum. Deputy Kovacs grabs the door frame and takes one last, quick look back into the darkness behind him.

Insert:

Deputy Kovacs' hand on the knob. A second hand, wearing brass knuckles, gently enfolds it.

Cut to Deputy Kovacs' face. He gasps.

EXT. ALLEY. NIGHT

The door hammers shut with a bang. Four of Deputy Kovacs' fingers, gripping the door frame, pop off at the knuckles all at once and fall down into a shallow puddle.

On the other side of the door, there is a scream of bloodcurdling agony, then a thump, a thwhack, and, finally, a wallop. Pause.

The door opens again. Jopling comes out in his stocking feet. He puts on his boots. He takes out a handkerchief, leans down and collects the four fingers off the ground, wraps them up, slips them into his pocket, and walks away down the alley.

INT. LOBBY. DAY

Eight a.m. Zero, substituting at the concierge desk again, looks up to the high window across the room. Herr Becker waits alone in the storage pantry with the ledger book under his arm. He checks his watch.

> MR. MOUSTAFA
> (voice-over)
> The next morning, Herr Becker received a peculiar, last-minute notice from the office of Deputy Kovacs: postponing their scheduled meeting – in perpetuity.

Title:

THREE DAYS LATER

EXT. VILLAGE. NIGHT

A nearly empty bus squeals to a stop behind a quiet inn in the middle of a deserted hamlet and deposits Zero on the roadside. He carries a knapsack and is dressed like a vagabond. The bus drives off.

Zero wanders to the middle of the cobblestone lane. He looks down at a rusty manhole. He looks up at the prison-castle across the way, high above the village. He checks his watch.

INT. CELL. NIGHT

M. Gustave, Pinky, Günther, Wolf, and Ludwig all lie quietly in their bunks with the sheets pulled up to their necks. Faraway voices shout and echo eerily. A guard walks through the section slamming doors and throwing bolts. With a series of loud thumps, block by block the lights go out, and the prison goes dark. Silence. Ludwig whispers:

LUDWIG

Let's blow!

The cell launches into soundless activity: bed linens are whisked away, the table is carried into the corner, and a row of floor-planks is carefully lifted. M. Gustave, Pinky, Günther, Wolf, and Ludwig are all dressed like vagabonds already and carry various sacks and baskets. One by one, they disappear into the floor. A pair of hands, at the rear, reaches up to replace the planks.

INT. CRAWL-SPACE. NIGHT

M. Gustave, Pinky, Günther, Wolf, and Ludwig advance on all fours, single file, through a low, moldy substructure.

INT. TOWER. NIGHT

A small window in a stone wall. Ludwig gently taps loose four pre-cut iron bars with one of the small hammers.

Insert:

The stump of one of the bars. A little noose is fitted over it and pulled tight.

Günther assists Ludwig as they slowly feed an unfurling tangle of rope and rungs out the window, inch by inch.

Cut to:

M. Gustave, Pinky, Günther, Wolf, and Ludwig all on the rope ladder at once like a string of beads dangling down the outside of the tower, 325 feet above the moat with crocodiles gliding along the dark surface. The ladder twists and creaks as they descend. Suddenly, a sharp voice calls out above their heads:

CONVICT
How'd *you* get out there?

They all look up. An anxious convict with a missing ear stares down at them from a cell window. Ludwig whispers:

LUDWIG
Shut up!

The convict frowns. He turns to his unseen bunkmates and says loudly:

CONVICT
These guys are tryin' to escape!

Ludwig looks furious. He whispers fiercely:

LUDWIG
What's wrong with you, you goddamn snitch?

CONVICT
(*hollering*)
Guard! Guard! They're gettin' away! They're –

A single, large hand grabs the convict with the missing ear by the neck, crushes the wind out of him, and rips him away from the window, out of view. Pause. The giant with the long scar across his face appears in the convict's place, looking down at the dangling escapees. M. Gustave says, gasping:

M. GUSTAVE
It's you! Thank you! Thank you, you sweet, kind man!

The giant nods sadly.

Cut to:

*The bottom of the rope ladder which ends halfway down the tower.
M. Gustave, Pinky, Günther, Wolf, and Ludwig step onto a narrow
ledge and make their way, sidestepping cautiously, around the
circumference of the building. They arrive at a small sloped roof and
open a trapdoor.*

INT. DORMITORY. NIGHT

*M. Gustave, Pinky, Günther, Wolf, and Ludwig all crouch on a beam
in the upper eaves of a vaulted hall. In the dark below, there are
twenty narrow cots in two rows. Next to each cot, there is a guard's
uniform on a coat-hanger, a billy-club on a peg, and a Luger pistol on
the night stand. Asleep in each cot, there is a lightly snoring goon.*

*Ludwig gets a firm grip on a tarnished copper pipe. He turns to the
others and nods. He swings out and makes his way, hand over hand,
from pipe to pipe across the ceiling. The others follow.*

INT. CELLAR. NIGHT

*A dirty chute sticks down from the ceiling above a wide garbage bin
filled with empty tins and rotting vegetables. M. Gustave, Pinky,
Günther, Wolf, and Ludwig slide down into view, one-by-one, drop out
into the trash pile, and hurry on their tiptoes into a dim corridor.*

Cut to:

*The candlelit dungeon. M. Gustave, Pinky, Günther, Wolf, and
Ludwig all listen attentively, looking up at the ceiling. There is a loud
but muffled sneeze above, then feet creaking away. Ludwig nods.*

*Pinky pulls away an oilskin tarp to reveal the cement pothole which
has now been chiselled all the way through the thick sub-floor clear
into the room below – where they see:*

*Three startled guards staring up at them from a card table in a dank,
brick basement. They each hold a hand of cards. One is in the middle
of placing a bet into a rich pot. A gas lantern flickers on a hook. The
escapees all cry out at once:*

LUDWIG

Whoa!

93

PINKY

Yow!

WOLF

Jeez!

M. GUSTAVE

Look out!

Günther whips the toothbrush-knife out of his sock and jumps down into the hole. The table shatters and cards and coins fly in every direction. There is a frenzy of punching, scrapping, and grunting. The others converge excitedly around the hole like the audience at a cock-fight. Günther kicks one guard in the teeth, slashes another across the neck, and socks the third, blasting the lantern into bits in the process.

The room goes black.

M. Gustave, Pinky, and Wolf cheer at a low decibel, whispering advice and encouragement simultaneously down into the darkness while Ludwig quickly searches for a match. He lights it and holds it over the hole.

Two of the guards are now sprawled out on their backs in a spreading pool of blood. Günther and the remaining guard twist and clutch on the floor, grappling in violent headlocks while they simultaneously stab each other repeatedly with the throat-slitter and a thick hunting knife. They both fall silent and stop moving. Silence. M. Gustave says quietly:

M. GUSTAVE

I suppose you'd call that a draw.

Ludwig sighs. He delivers a brief eulogy:

LUDWIG

Anyway, he went out with a bloody knife in his fist jammed into the gut of a dyin' prison guard. I think that's how he would've wanted it, don't you?

M. Gustave, Pinky, and Wolf nod and solemnly concur, muttering. They climb down into the hole.

EXT. STREET. NIGHT

Zero watches as the manhole cover flips open onto the street. M. Gustave pokes his head up and whispers simply:

M. GUSTAVE

Good evening.

Zero rushes to assist M. Gustave out of the storm drain. Pinky, Wolf, and Ludwig surface on high alert, looking around in every direction. (Pinky carries a wad of the crumbled-up gambling money in his little hand.)

M. GUSTAVE

Let me introduce you. Pinky, Wolf, and Ludwig: this is the divine Zero. (*Soberly to Zero.*) Günther was slain in the catacombs.

M. Gustave crosses himself quickly. He begins a wistful speech:

Well, boys, who knows when we'll all meet again; but *if*, one day –

LUDWIG

No time to gab. Take care of yourself, Mr. Gustave. Good luck, kid.

Pinky, Wolf, and Ludwig sprint away into the woods. M. Gustave watches them go, bittersweet. He grabs Zero by the shoulder and says, suddenly urgent:

M. GUSTAVE

Which way to the safe house?

ZERO
(*unfortunately*)

I couldn't find one.

M. GUSTAVE
(*in disbelief*)

No *safe* house? Really? We're completely on our own out here?

ZERO
(*worried*)

I'm afraid so. I asked around, but I didn't want to take any chances. I thought . . .

Zero trails off. He looks apologetic. M. Gustave sighs, resigned. He says calmly:

95

M. GUSTAVE

I understand. Too risky. We'll just have to wing it, I suppose. Let's put on our disguises.

Zero hesitates. He looks down at his vagabond costume, then at M. Gustave's. He says, confused:

ZERO

We're *wearing* them.

M. GUSTAVE
(*frustrated*)
No, we're not. We said false *whiskers* and fake *noses* and so on. You didn't bring any?

ZERO
(*referring to moustache*)
I thought you were *growing* one. It wouldn't look realistic, would it? I thought . . .

Zero trails off again. He deflates, distressed. M. Gustave remains calm.

M. GUSTAVE
When done properly, they're perfectly convincing – but I take your point. So be it. Give me a few squirts of *L'Air de Panache*, please, will you?

Zero smacks his hand to his forehead and looks mortified. M. Gustave says bluntly:

M. GUSTAVE
Can I not get a squirt, even?

ZERO
(*miserably*)
I forgot the *L'Air de Panache*.

M. GUSTAVE
(*at peak frustration*)
Honestly – you *forgot* the *L'Air de Panache*? I don't *believe* it. How *could* you? I've been in jail. Zero! Do you understand how humiliating this is? I *smell*.

M. Gustave lifts up his arms. Zero sniffs him. He grimaces. M. Gustave's eyes narrow. He begins to seethe.

Well, that's just marvelous, isn't it? I suppose this is to be expected back in – where do you come from, again?

ZERO
(*evenly*)

Aq Salim al-Jabat.

M. GUSTAVE
(*escalating*)

Precisely. I suppose this is to be expected back in Aq Salim al-Jabat where one's prized possessions are a stack of filthy carpets and a starving goat, and one sleeps behind a tent-flap and survives on wild dates and scarabs – but it's not how *I* trained you. What on God's earth possessed you to leave the homeland where you very obviously belong and travel unspeakable distances to become a penniless immigrant in a refined, highly cultivated society that, quite frankly, could've gotten along very well without you?

ZERO
(*shrugs*)

The war.

M. GUSTAVE
(*pause*)

Say again?

Zero speaks softly and struggles deliberately to hold back his emotions as he says, staring at the ground:

ZERO

Well, you see, my father was murdered, and the rest of my family were executed by firing squad. Our village was burned to the ground. Those who managed to survive were forced to flee. I left – because of the war.

M. GUSTAVE
(*back-peddling*)

Ah, I see. So you're, actually, really more of a refugee, in that sense.

ZERO
(*reserved*)

Truly.

M. GUSTAVE
(*ashamed*)

Well, I suppose I'd better take back everything I just said.
What a bloody idiot I am. Pathetic *fool*. Goddamn selfish
bastard. This is disgraceful – and it's beneath the standards
of the Grand Budapest.

*Zero looks increasingly concerned as M. Gustave begins to come
unglued. Tears stream down M. Gustave's face. He stands at attention
and says with deep deference:*

I apologize on behalf of the hotel.

ZERO
(*gently*)

It's not your fault, M. Gustave. You were just upset I forgot
the perfume.

M. GUSTAVE

Don't make excuses for me. I owe you my *life*.

*M. Gustave takes Zero by the hand. He says with great feeling and
sincerity:*

You're my *dear* friend and protégé, and I'm *very* proud of
you. You *must* know that. I'm so sorry, Zero.

ZERO
(*gallantly*)

We're *brothers*.

*M. Gustave, touched to the quick, instantly kisses Zero on both cheeks
and they embrace. They release each other. They try to pull themselves
back together. Pause.*

M. GUSTAVE

How's our darling Agatha?

Zero starts to answer, then hesitates. He recites:

ZERO

''Twas first light when I saw her face upon the heath; and
hence did I return, day by day, entranc'd: tho' vinegar did
brine my heart –'

A powerful siren begins to blast across the region. Zero's eyes dart around, startled. M. Gustave says over the noise, impressed:

> M. GUSTAVE
>
> *Very* good! I'm going to stop you because the alarm has sounded – but remember where we left off, because I *insist* you finish later!

M. Gustave and Zero take off full speed down the road.

INT. TELEPHONE BOOTH. NIGHT

A black-and-yellow wooden call-box next to a tiny pub outside the village. Windmills spin gently on the far side of a wheat field in the distance. Zero holds the door open while M. Gustave dials.

> M. GUSTAVE
>
> Operator, get me the Excelsior Palace in Baden-Jürgen and reverse the charges, please. (*To Zero.*) We've no choice. There's nowhere else to turn. (*Into the receiver.*) I'll hold. Thank you. (*To Zero.*) It's our only hope. Otherwise, I shouldn't even mention its existence to you. It goes without saying, you must never breath a word about this to a living soul. Do you swear?

> ZERO
>
> Of course. What *is* it, in fact?

> M. GUSTAVE
>
> I can't say. (*Into the receiver.*) *Guten Abend. M. Ivan, bitte. Danke.* (*By way of explanation, to Zero.*) How does one come by front-row aisle seats for a first night at the Opera Toscana with one day's notice? How does one arrange a private viewing of the tapestry collection at the Royal Saxon Gallery? How does one secure a corner table at Chez Dominique on a *Thursday?*

Zero nods as he takes this in, intrigued. Pause. M. Gustave says suddenly into the receiver, turning on the charm:

> Ivan, darling, it's Gustave! Hello! Well, I *was* until about five minutes ago. We've taken it upon ourselves to clear out in a

hurry, if you see what I mean. Through a sewer, as it happens. Exactly! Listen, Ivan, sorry to cut you off, but we're in a bit of a bind. This is an official request. (*Officially.*) I'm formally calling upon the special services of –

Title:

PART 4:
'THE SOCIETY OF THE CROSSED KEYS'

INT. FIRST LOBBY. NIGHT

Concierge desk No.1. There are rows of mailboxes with room numbers on them, keys on hooks, and a bell on the counter-top. A slim concierge with a long moustache talks on the telephone. He is M. Ivan. A lobby boy waits beside him silently.

M. IVAN

I'll call you back, Gustave. Right. Stand by.

M. Ivan hangs up the telephone and turns to a waiting young couple as he produces a small paper map from a drawer.

I beg your pardon. Do you prefer to walk? We're right here.

M. Ivan makes a little 'X' in ink on the map. He draws a line.

It's very simple. Straight down the corniche. Then left. (*To the lobby boy.*) Jojo, see them out.

The young couple take the map gratefully, and the lobby boy escorts them away. M. Ivan picks up the telephone again and says urgently:

Get me M. Georges at the Château Luxe, please.

Cut to:

The dining room at a hunting lodge. One hundred small children crowd around a long table. There is a huge birthday cake with seven lit candles on it. Streamers hang from the ceiling. Balloons float on strings. A very tall, bony concierge conducts the room singing 'Happy Birthday'. He is M. Georges.

A lobby boy goes over to M. Georges and whispers in his ear. M. Georges nods and quickly exits. The lobby boy replaces him and takes over the conducting.

INT. SECOND LOBBY. NIGHT

Concierge desk No. 2. M. Georges picks up the telephone.

> M. GEORGES
> Hello, Ivan? You don't say? Is he really? How about that?
> Got it.

M. Georges presses down on the hook to disconnect, then lifts it up again and says urgently:

> M. GEORGES
> Get me M. Dino at the Palazzo Principessa, please.

Cut to:

A busy piazza across from a church. There is a crowded trattoria on the sidewalk. There is a statue of a centurion. One hundred men and women in pajamas and bathrobes stand on the street in front of a hotel looking up at a fourth-floor window with smoke gushing out of it while a ladder extends from a fire engine toward a calm old woman at the window sill. An alarm rings loudly. A stocky concierge with slick, black hair stands at the front of the crowd yelling orders and holding a fire extinguisher. He is M. Dino.

A lobby boy goes over to M. Reggio and whispers in his ear. M. Dino nods and quickly goes into the hotel. The lobby boy takes the fire extinguisher and replaces him yelling orders.

INT. THIRD LOBBY. NIGHT

Concierge desk No. 3. The lobby is a bit smoky. M. Dino picks up the telephone.

> M. DINO
> M. Georges. No trouble at all. Tell me. I see. I see. Straight
> away.

M. Dino presses down on the hook to disconnect, then lifts it up again and says urgently:

> M. DINO
> Get me M. Robin at L'Hôtel Côte du Cap, please.

Cut to:

A clay tennis court overlooking a bright blue sea at sunset. Twenty-five men and women in tennis whites and bathing suits circle around another tennis player lying flat on his back on the ground while a very fit, sporty concierge with a pompadour sits on one knee next to him checking his pulse. He is M. Robin.

A lobby boy goes over to M. Robin and whispers in his ear. M. Robin nods and quickly leaves the court. The lobby boy replaces him and resumes checking the fallen man's pulse.

INT. FOURTH LOBBY. NIGHT

Concierge desk No. 4. M. Robin picks up the telephone.

> M. ROBIN
> This is M. Robin. Yes, Dino. Yes, Dino. Yes, Dino. OK,
> Dino.

M. Robin presses down on the hook to disconnect, then lifts it up again and says urgently:

> M. ROBIN
> Get me M. Martin at the Ritz Imperial, please.

Cut to:

An extremely busy hotel kitchen filled with cooks of every rank and specialty. Waiters dash in and out continuously. A small, round concierge with a pink face is screaming and pointing a serving fork at the chef, who is flambé-ing a crêpe Suzette). He is M. Martin.

A lobby boy goes over to M. Martin and whispers in his ear. M. Martin nods and quickly exits the kitchen. The lobby boy takes the serving fork and replaces him screaming at the chef.

INT. FIFTH LOBBY. NIGHT

Concierge desk No. 5. M. Martin picks up the telephone.

> M. MARTIN
> Robin, Martin. I know. So I heard. (*Suddenly intrigued.*) Maybe. (*Gravely.*) Let me make a few calls.

EXT. WHEAT FIELD. NIGHT

M. Gustave and Zero wait hidden behind a haystack next to the telephone booth. M. Gustave recaps:

> M. GUSTAVE
> Serge X: missing. Deputy Kovacs: also missing. Madame D.: dead. 'Boy with Apple': stolen (by us). Dmitri and Jopling: ruthless, cold-blooded savages. Gustave H: at large. What else?

> ZERO
> Zero: confused.

> M. GUSTAVE
> (*nodding*)
> Zero: confused, indeed. The plot 'thickens', as they say. Why, by the way? Is it a soup metaphor?

> ZERO
> I don't know.

Distant tires squeal.

M. Gustave and Zero sit up quickly and peer off down the road. An approaching car accelerates, whining in the darkness. A pair of headlights pops into view from the woods. A large sedan emerges with a roar, zig-zagging onto the farm road. It slides across the gravel and rips to a stop in front of them. A sign next to five stars on the side of the hood reads: HOTEL EXCELSIOR PALACE.

One of the back doors snaps open, and M. Ivan shouts from inside:

M. IVAN

Get in!

M. Gustave and Zero dash out from behind the haystack and sprint to the vehicle.

INT. HOTEL CAR. DAY

The door slams shut, and the chauffeur punches it. They speed back into the hamlet. M. Ivan immediately begins briefing M. Gustave and Zero:

M. IVAN

We found the butler. He's hiding out in the remote foothills near Gabelmeister's Peak. Our contact convinced him to meet you midday tomorrow at the observatory on the summit. Tell no one. He'll explain everything. The train departs in four and a half minutes. Here's your tickets.

M. Ivan deals out a pair of train tickets to M. Gustave and Zero. M. Gustave gives his a quick study, then mumbles a puzzled objection:

M. GUSTAVE

Third class?

M. IVAN

It was overbooked, but the conductor used to be a *sommelier* at the old Versailles. He pulled some strings. You'll need these for the dining car.

M. Ivan produces two, pre-tied neckties. M. Gustave and Zero slip them over their heads and adjust the knots. The chauffeur hits the brakes, and M. Ivan swings the door open again.

M. IVAN

Go!

EXT. TRAIN STATION. NIGHT

M. Gustave and Zero jump out in front of a very small depot and slam the door. M. Ivan says out the window:

> M. IVAN
>
> One last thing.

M. Ivan leans down and searches for something on the floor. He sits up and thrusts out a tiny version of a familiar bottle. M. Gustave melts as he realizes:

> M. GUSTAVE
>
> *L'Air de Panache*!

> M. IVAN
> (*downplaying it*)
> They only had the half-ounce.

M. Gustave looks impressed and deeply touched. He leans to Zero and whispers:

> M. GUSTAVE
>
> We should give him something as a symbolic gesture. How much money you got?

> ZERO
> (*hesitates*)
> Forty-two Klubecks and three postage stamps.

> M. GUSTAVE
>
> Give me twenty-five.

Zero's eyes widen. He cocks his head, dubious. M. Gustave nods firmly. Zero reluctantly digs a handful of coins and bills out of his pocket and passes it onto M. Gustave. M. Gustave says to M. Ivan with profound gratitude:

> M. GUSTAVE
>
> Bless you.

M. Gustave attempts to discreetly press the money into M. Ivan's palm – but M. Ivan withdraws. He waves his hands and says by way of gentle refusal:

Please.

M. Gustave smiles sadly. He bows. The hotel car skids away.

Silence. M. Gustave sprays himself four times with the perfume atomizer. His posture and bearing immediately improve. He turns to Zero. Pause.

M. Gustave holds out the bottle. Zero looks confused – then simultaneously flattered and hesitant. He takes the cologne and spritzes himself once lightly. He gives a polite nod and returns the bottle.

A train pulls into the station, and M. Gustave and Zero race out onto the platform.

Cut to:

A stack of wooden planks next to the opening in the cell floor. Ten guards and twenty soldiers stand crowded in the little room looking down at the hole. Henckel's head pokes up from the crawl-space below. He wears a look of grim determination as he delivers the following:

> HENCKELS
> I want road blocks at every junction for fifty kilometers. I want *rail* blocks at every train station for a hundred kilometers. I want fifty men and ten bloodhounds ready in five minutes. We're going to strip-search every *pretzel-haus, waffelhut, biergarten* – and *especially* every grand hotel – from Augenzburg to Zilchbrück. These men are dangerous, professional criminals. (At least, three of them are, anyway.)

Henckels hesitates. He squints across the room. He points.

> Who are *you*?

The guards and soldiers all turn to look past the bunks behind them and clear the view to:

Jopling alone in the dim back corner.

> What are you doing here? Civilian personnel aren't permitted in the cell block. This is a military investigation.

Jopling steps fully into view. A shifty guard explains nervously:

This is Mr. Jopling, sir. His employer's mother was one of the victims of the –

HENCKELS

Shut up.

Henckels climbs up out of the hole as Jopling approaches and offers his card. Henckel snaps it up, gives it a fraction-of-a-second look, then hands it off to an underling.

You work for the family Desgoffe und Taxis?

Pause. Jopling nods. Henckels asks pointedly:

Are you aware of the murder of Deputy Vilmos Kovacs on the twenty-third of October?

JOPLING
(*carefully*)
I'm aware of his disappearance.

> HENCKELS

His body was found stuffed in a sarcophagus behind a storage room at the Kunstmuseum late last night. He was short four fingers. What do you say about *that*?

Henckels withdraws a typewritten document out of his coat. He holds it up.

Insert:

A police report with a photograph of Deputy Kovacs' body in a Pharaoh's casket with his hands crossed on his chest. A section at the bottom of the page is labeled FINGERPRINTS. *There are five for the left hand, but only a thumb for the right.*

Jopling studies the document. He shrugs.

> HENCKELS

Escort Mr. Jopling off the premises.

Jopling makes his way toward the cell door accompanied by several soldiers. He pauses just before he exits. He leans down and picks up a flattened, pink cardboard box off the floor. He scrapes a ridge of icing with his finger and licks the tip. He says softly:

> JOPLING

Mendl's.

Henckels watches Jopling suspiciously as he shrinks away down the corridor.

INT. LIBRARY. NIGHT

Dmitri, dressed in black pajamas and a black smoking jacket with a fur collar, listens on the telephone in a small alcove. He says calmly:

> DMITRI

Talk to his club-footed sister again – and, this time: be persuasive.

Dmitri hangs up. He crosses into the library and stands in front of a snooker table. The box containing Madame D.'s will sits among billiard balls in the middle of it. Its contents have been spread out and scattered

into a sprawling mess. *Marguerite, Laetizia, and Carolina play cards and sip at tiny glasses of port at the other end of the room.*

Dmitri drinks a vodka in one gulp. He shuffles and sifts among the scraps, preoccupied. He picks up a folded sliver of cream-colored writing paper. He opens it.

Insert:

A page of Grand Budapest Hotel stationery with a set of crossed keys insignia at the top. Handwritten below is: 'Remember: I'm always with you.'

Dmitri stares at the piece of paper. He tosses it back onto the table. It lands on top of a faded, old photograph of 'Boy with Apple' with the stamp at the bottom of a long defunct auction house.

Dmitri frowns. He turns around and looks up at the wall above the fireplace directly behind him. His face goes white.

Cut to:

The woodcut print of the two lesbians masturbating. A bit of the discolored wallpaper sticks out behind it on either side.

Dmitri is stunned. He stammers:

> DMITRI
> Holy fuck! What's the meaning of this shit?

Marguerite, Laetizia, and Carolina all look. They seem confused. They respond simultaneously:

> MARGUERITE
> 'Boy with Apple'? I thought you'd *hidden* it.

> LAETIZIA
> It's been missing two weeks. I assumed it went to the tax-appraiser.

> CAROLINA
> Why are you only noticing now?

Dmitri shakes his head, speechless. He says finally, in angry shock:

> DMITRI
> Are you fucking kidding me?

Clotilde has materialized. Dmitri turns to her. Marguerite, Laetizia, and Carolina turn to her, also. Clotilde's voice cracks and quivers as she says:

> CLOTIDE
> I believe it was removed by M. Gustave.

Pause. Dmitri grabs the woodcut off the wall and slams it (punching a thick hole through the center) over a small marble discus-thrower.

INT. TRAIN CAR. NIGHT

A third-class compartment on the overnight to Gabelmeister's Peak. Students, peasants, and laborers sleep among rucksacks and baskets on hard benches and shelves lining the walls. M. Gustave and Zero whisper to each other from their bunks near the ceiling on either side of the room:

M. GUSTAVE

I'm not *angry* with Serge. You can't *blame* someone for their basic lack of moral fiber. He's a frightened, little, yellow-bellied coward. That's not *his* fault, is it?

ZERO

I don't know. It depends.

M. GUSTAVE
(*irritated*)

Well, you can say that about most anything. 'It depends.' Of course it depends.

ZERO
(*firmly*)

Of course it depends.

M. GUSTAVE
(*sighs*)

Yes, I suppose you're right. Of course, it depends. However: that doesn't mean I'm not going to throttle the little swamp rat. (*Pause.*) May I officiate, by the way? The ceremony.

ZERO
(*surprised, humbly*)

With pleasure.

M. Gustave sighs. He says with deep sincerity and feeling:

M. GUSTAVE

I must say, I find that girl utterly delightful. Flat as a board, enormous birthmark the shape of Mexico over half her face, sweating for hours on end in that sweltering kitchen while Mendl (genius though he is) looms over her like a hulking gorilla – yet without question, without fail, always, and invariably: she's *exceedingly* lovely. Why? Because of her purity.

ZERO
(*pleased*)

She admires you, as well, M. Gustave.

> M. GUSTAVE
> (*perking up*)

Does she?

> ZERO

Very much.

> M. GUSTAVE
> (*impressed*)

That's a good sign, you know. It means she 'gets it'. That's important.

> ZERO
> (*pause*)

Don't flirt with her.

M. Gustave scoffs, irritated.

INT. GARRET. NIGHT

Agatha's room. Her few possessions are laid out neatly on the mattress: two changes of clothes, a short stack of cookbooks, her volume of romantic poetry, some tangled ribbons, and a hairbrush.

Agatha reaches up to the top of a skinny, pine wardrobe and pulls down an old, wicker suitcase. It has been repaired extensively with wire and string. She transfers everything she owns into it swiftly. She buckles it shut, slides it under the bed – then bolts upright. She looks up at the ceiling.

There is a thump.

Silence. Agatha slips off her shoes (wooden clogs). She slowly steps up onto the bed. She stands on her tiptoes.

EXT. ROOF. NIGHT

There is no moon, and the night is pitch-black. Agatha's hands grip the edges of the skylight's frame. Her eyes come up into view. She looks cautiously around in every direction. She listens.

Agatha sinks back down, pulls away the pencil holding the skylight window open, and quickly latches it shut.

The camera holds on the empty rooftop: a quiet wind whistles over the sleeping village.

Insert:

The front page of the Trans-Alpine Yodel. *Headline:*

YOUNG GIRL'S HEAD FOUND IN LAUNDRY BASKET

INT. COMMAND HEADQUARTERS. DAY

The next morning. An office decorated with flags, shields, and swords. There is a large map on a broad table with game pieces (chess, checkers, jacks, dice, and dominoes) marking troops and munitions. Henckels sits in a leather armchair drinking a cup of coffee while he stares at the front page of the newspaper.

A First Lieutenant stands over him holding a notebook and an envelope labeled WIRE MESSAGE. *He explains:*

LIEUTENANT

A radio telegram was delivered and signed for by the girl at four a.m. The envelope was found near the body, but its contents were missing – however: the telegraph office always keeps a carbon of the ticker-tape for twenty-four hours. I copied it down. It reads as follows: 'Pack your things stop be ready to leave at moment's notice stop hide-out is vicinity of Gabelmeister's Peak stop destroy this message all my love full stop.'

HENCKELS
(pause)

Where's the basket?

The Lieutenant points across the room. Henckels sighs. He stands up and walks over to a laundry basket on top of a desk against the wall. Pause. He reaches into it and lifts out, by the hair:

Serge's sister's severed head.

Title:

PART 5: 'GABELMEISTER'S PEAK'

Insert:

The radio telegram – which has been torn to shreds, then carefully taped back together. It is speckled with blood.

EXT. GAS STATION. DAY

A lone fuel-pump in front of a service shack at the foot of a hill on a snowy country road. A fourteen-year-old Pump Attendant in a greasy jumpsuit fills the tank of Jopling's motorcycle. A sled-runner has been fitted over the front wheel.

Jopling leans against the wall, silent, looking down at the radio telegram in his hands. The Pump Attendant chirps:

> PUMP ATTENDANT
> Where you headed, mister?

Pause. Jopling's eyeballs turn to the attendant.

> PUMP ATTENDANT
> Skiing? Sledding? Mountain climbing?

Jopling looks away again.

The Pump Attendant grows slightly uneasy. Jopling reaches into his leather coat – half revealing, holstered, inside: a stiletto icepick, a blackjack bludgeon, a Luger pistol, and a ball-peen hammer. He withdraws a glass flask with a silver stopper and takes a pull. His brass knuckles clack against it.

The Pump Attendant clears his throat, pulls the nozzle out of the tank, and says – polite but quick:

> PUMP ATTENDANT
> Three Klubecks, please.

EXT. TRAIN STATION. DAY

The Zubrowkian Alps. A high-altitude depot nestled in a pass between two craggy ridges. There is fresh powder on the ground. Scattered flakes flicker in the air. A sign along the tracks reads: 'Gabelmeister's Peak'.

Twenty-five soldiers armed with carbine rifles stand spaced apart down the length of the platform, waiting.

The train rolls in. Doors open, and passengers with skis, snow-shoes, and suitcases step down and hurry into the building and around its sides. The soldiers study them, attentive, and peer inside the compartment windows. The passengers continue until they have all cleared away, and the platform is quiet again. A train conductor, leaning out from the end of a car, watches the soldiers. The soldiers look to each other tentatively.

A Sergeant jerks open a door and steps onto the train. He looks around. He raises his chin, lifts his nose – and sniffs the air. He looks irritated.

EXT. OBSERVATORY. DAY

The peak of an icy butte. A narrow, domed building sticks up into the sky at the top. A steel balcony winds around it with a platform that extends out over a plunging drop into the white mist. A group of scientists bundled in fur coats listens to a professor. A man on a bench pours cocoa from a Thermos. An eagle circles overhead.

M. Gustave and Zero shiver at the end of the railing.

> M. GUSTAVE
> It's a hell of a view. I give them that, for what it's worth.

> ZERO
> I agree.

Pause. M. Gustave checks his watch. He says with a slightly bitter edge to his voice:

> M. GUSTAVE
> When one says 'midday' – what does that mean to you?

> ZERO
> High noon.

> M. GUSTAVE
> Exactly. In other words, twelve p.m. At least, that's always been *my* interpretation.

Silence. M. Gustave withdraws the small bottle of cologne from his pocket, spritzes himself twice, hands it to Zero who does the same automatically, then tucks it back away again. He holds out his palm under the flittering snow. He begins to recite:

M. GUSTAVE

''Tis oft-remarked: no single, falling flake does any other in its pure and perfect form –'

ZERO
(*tensely*)

Somebody's coming.

A Monk in a grey cloak and a thick scarf clanks up a metal staircase. His face is old and wrinkled. He walks directly out to M. Gustave and Zero and stops. He studies them for a moment, frowning. He whispers:

MONK I

Are you M. Gustave of the Grand Budapest Hotel in Nebelsbad?

M. GUSTAVE
(*hesitates*)

Uh-huh.

MONK I

Get on the next cable car.

The Monk points.

A cable car is just arriving down the sloping line from an adjacent peak. M. Gustave hesitates. The Monk urges him on with a brusque motion. M. Gustave and Zero sprint across the balcony, scramble down a flight of steps, and race out onto the boarding platform. A family of six waits in skiing costumes. They stare at M. Gustave and Zero as they arrive, breathless. A tramway operator holds open the door. Everyone boards, squeezing.

INT. AERIAL TRAM. DAY

The cable car sets off up and across the wide ravine. M. Gustave and Zero sit side by side with the curious, silent family. The father sniffs the air. He looks irritated.

116

Halfway there: the cable car slams to a stop with a clunk.

Everyone is startled. The stalled vehicle sways in the quiet wind. The father looks up. The mother looks down. The children look to each other. In the distance: there is a faint, mechanical hum. M. Gustave and Zero look out.

Another cable car is ascending at a diagonal on a different line. They all watch as it slowly approaches. Just as it is about to criss-cross their path, it slams to a stop, too.

Another elderly, cloaked Monk stares out from inside the other cable car. He is alone in the vehicle. He studies M. Gustave and Zero for a moment, frowning. He whispers loudly:

MONK 2

Are you M. Gustave of the Grand Budapest Hotel in Nebelsbad?

M. GUSTAVE
(*hesitates*)

Uh-huh.

MONK 2

Switch with me.

The Monk unlatches the door of his cable car and opens it. The family watch nervously as M. Gustave and Zero stand up, rocking the vehicle, open their own door, and carefully exit. They reluctantly lunge across the precarious abyss. The Monk changes places with them. There is another clunk, and the two cable cars resume their journeys.

M. Gustave and Zero exchange a look. Their new cable car continues up toward its destination. A sign above the arrival platform reads: 'Our Holy Father of the Sudetenwaltz'. Directly below it, there is a walled fort with a steeple and a tall stone cross.

Another tramway attendant holds the door open for them as they disembark.

EXT. MONASTERY. DAY

M. Gustave and Zero walk down a staircase and through the front gate into an empty churchyard. There are walls and low buildings on the sides, a few graves in the middle, and the entrance to a church at one end. Pause.

A small window swings open next to M. Gustave and Zero. Another elderly, cloaked Monk stares out from inside a caretaker's booth. He studies them for a moment, frowning. He whispers:

> MONK 3
>
> Are you M. Gustave of the Grand Budapest Hotel in Nebelsbad?

> M. GUSTAVE
> (hesitates)
>
> Uh-huh.

> MONK 3
>
> Put these on and sing.

The Monk thrusts a small bundle into M. Gustave's hands. It consists of: two cloaks and two hymnals. The echoing sound of a Gregorian chant begins to rise from all around. M. Gustave and Zero swiftly slip on the cloaks just as a procession of a hundred monks enters from two directions, merges in the churchyard, and advances double-file toward the chapel.

M. Gustave and Zero open their hymnals at random and slip into the procession.

INT. CHURCH. DAY

A blasting organ joins the chant inside a vast, austere hall as the procession enters. The Monks file into pews. The music ends, and the room goes silent. Everyone kneels. The monsignor at the altar places his hands on a thick Bible and speaks Latin.

A voice behind M. Gustave and Zero says:

> MONK 4
>
> Psst.

M. Gustave and Zero turn around. Another elderly, cloaked monk kneels on a kneeler behind them with his hands folded in prayer. He studies them for a moment, frowning. He whispers:

MONK 4

Are you M. Gustave of the –

M. GUSTAVE
(*irritated*)

Yes, dammit.

MONK 4

Confess.

M. Gustave looks deeply offended and flabbergasted. He snaps:

M. GUSTAVE

I'm *innocent.*

MONK 4
(*annoyed*)

No, no.

The Monk points to a confessional booth in the transept.

M. Gustave hesitates. He nods, realizing. He and Zero look down the row of kneeling legs. They step up onto the pew, slink quickly in a crouch to the aisle, then hop down to the floor. Monks, watching them, frown.

M. Gustave and Zero hurry together into the confessional booth and close the door.

INT. CONFESSIONAL. DAY

A dark, wooden box lined with purple velvet. It is a bit tight for two. A panel slides open. Through the lattice screen: Serge has aged a decade. His eyes are watery and dim. He whispers immediately, reverent:

SERGE

Forgive me, M. Gustave. I never meant to betray you. They threatened my life, and now they've murdered my only family.

M. GUSTAVE
(*frustrated*)

No! Who'd they kill this time?

SERGE

(*deeply wounded*)

My dear sister.

M. GUSTAVE

(*trying to picture her*)

The girl with the club-foot?

SERGE

Yes.

M. GUSTAVE

Those *fuckers*.

SERGE

I tried to warn you. At the beginning.

M. GUSTAVE

I know, darling. Let's put that behind us. Listen: I hate to put you on the spot, but I really must ask you to clear my name. Obviously, you're *grieving*, and if I had any other –

SERGE

There's more.

M. GUSTAVE

(*hesitates*)

OK.

SERGE

To the story.

M. GUSTAVE

I get it. Go on.

SERGE

I was the official witness in Madame D.'s presence to the creation of a second will to be executed only in the event of her death by murder.

M. GUSTAVE

A second will.

SERGE

Right.

M. GUSTAVE

In case she got bumped off.

SERGE

Right.

M. GUSTAVE

Uh-huh?

SERGE

But they destroyed it.

M. GUSTAVE

Oh, dear.

SERGE

However.

M. GUSTAVE

Uh-huh?

SERGE

I pulled a copy.

                    M. GUSTAVE
                     (*beat*)
    A second copy of the second will.

                      SERGE
     Right.

                    M. GUSTAVE
     Uh-huh?

Long pause. M. Gustave finally starts to lose his composure. His voice rises:

                    M. GUSTAVE
     Well, what does it say? Where is it? What's it all about,
     dammit? Don't keep us in suspense, Serge. This has been
     a complete fucking nightmare. Just tell us what the fuck is
     going on!

The panel snaps shut. M. Gustave and Zero frown. The organ blasts again outside the confessional, and the church booms with low, eerie, singing voices. M. Gustave tries to jerk the panel open, but it sticks. He bangs on it with his fists.

                    M. GUSTAVE
     Serge? Serge? Serge!

M. Gustave tries the door. It is locked. Zero peers at the keyhole and says shortly:

                      ZERO
     Give me the pass-keys.

M. Gustave hesitates. He reaches into his pocket and pulls out his ring of Grand Budapest pass keys. Zero rapidly flips through them, studying each key. He settles on one, inserts it into the keyhole, jiggles it, and twists. The lock clicks.

Cut to:

M. Gustave and Zero jumping out from the confessional booth. Zero darts to the other side and cracks open the other door. He peeks in and sees:

Serge with a bloody garrote-wire strung around his neck. His eyes are wide open, and his tongue sticks out slightly.

Zero grimaces. M. Gustave looks over his shoulder.

M. GUSTAVE

Bloody *hell*. They've strangled the poor slob!

M. Gustave presses the door quietly shut again. He and Zero both look frantically around the room.

One lone Monk swings a smoking censer as he recesses quickly down the center aisle while the rest of the congregation stand in their pews singing. He steps outside and ducks away around the corner.

M. Gustave's and Zero's eyes light up – then narrow fiercely.

EXT. COURTYARD. DAY

M. Gustave and Zero dash out the front doors. They skid to a stop and scan the area. There is a display next to the church entrance of a wooden saint on a sled being pulled by a papier-mâché *reindeer. There is no one else in sight.*

A door creaks slowly in the wind outside a small shed across the way. A sign above it reads: 'Ski Locker (Clerical Use Only)'. A cloak and the still-smoldering censer are strewn in the snow in front of it.

Insert:

A pair of high-heeled boots clamping into a pair of ski-clips.

Insert:

A pair of hands with brass knuckles gripping a pair of ski-poles.

Cut to:

Jopling (without cloak, on skis) exploding out the door of the shed, making a hard pivot, and launching through the monastery gate, down the steep slope.

M. Gustave and Zero watch in shock.

Zero turns to the display next to them. He leaps over to it, kicks off the saint, flips away the reindeer, and shoves the sled full speed across the churchyard. He shouts:

ZERO

Come on!

M. Gustave chases after Zero, and they jump on board just as the sled dips sharply and accelerates like mad down the mountain. Zero hangs onto a short rope knotted to the front. M. Gustave hangs onto Zero.

Jopling, skiing superbly up ahead, looks back. He sees M. Gustave and Zero closing in. He frowns. He makes a quick detour through a gap in the trees and races down a narrow, zig-zag path.

Zero jerks the rope and follows Jopling. The sled bounces and bumps, skids and slides. Zero shouts:

> ZERO
> What do we do if we catch him?

> M. GUSTAVE
> (*pause*)
> I don't know! He's a homicidal psychopath! Let's stop!

> ZERO
> I can't! I can barely *steer*!

Jopling ramps over the sloped roof of a shuttered café and lands cleanly. M. Gustave and Zero duck and shoot under it, banging between tables, scattering chairs, and rattling off the terrace.

A group of hikers in snow-shoes walks single file across the slope. They hurry to one side in a panic to dodge Jopling, then immediately hurry back to the other to dodge M. Gustave and Zero.

A long, paper banner rustles in the wind. It reads: GABELMEISTER'S PEAK, WINTER GAMES. *Jopling snaps through it and shoots out onto an abandoned bobsled run. He balances nimbly as he rockets down the ice. M. Gustave and Zero burst onto the track behind him, skittering through the corners. They grit their teeth and hang on, terrified.*

At the end of the run, Jopling jolts sideways, scratching across the track and showering splinters of ice, then zips up into the air and lands on the snow at the side of a road directly next to his parked motorcycle. He watches as:

M. Gustave and Zero come flying down the bobsled run at breakneck speed, slam into a dense bank at the bottom, and soar into a high arc. The sled flips and twirls, then hits the ground and splits into three pieces. Zero bashes headfirst into the deep snow and disappears – except

*for his feet and ankles sticking out into the air, motionless. M. Gustave
smacks onto the ice and slides, spinning, off the edge of a cliff. Silence.*

*Jopling takes a drink from his flask. He unclips his skis. He walks
slowly past Zero's frozen legs and approaches the precipice.*

*M. Gustave is clutching onto a knob of jagged ice while his feet dangle
above a rocky chasm a thousand feet deep. He stares up at Jopling,
frightened but furious. He says quietly:*

M. GUSTAVE
You sick, pathetic *creep.* I hate you. (*Shouting.*) Run, Zero!
Save yourself, I suppose!

Zero's feet are frozen in place. A distant wolf howls. Pause.

*Jopling lifts his foot and stomps his boot down with all his might. The
ice crackles and fissures. M. Gustave sighs miserably. He swallows.
Jopling stomps again. The ice around M. Gustave begins to crumble.
As Jopling continues to stomp, over and over, M. Gustave sadly recites:*

M. GUSTAVE
'"If this do be me end: farewell!" cried the wounded piper-
boy, whilst the muskets cracked and the yeomen roared,

"Hurrah!" and the ramparts fell. "Methinks me breathes me last, me fears!" said he –'

There is a powerful thump, and Jopling flies headfirst, screaming, off the cliff over M. Gustave's head. Zero, in the midst of a diving shove, lands on his face and nearly goes over the edge himself. He is covered with snow. M. Gustave shouts, ecstatic:

M. GUSTAVE

Holy shit! You *got* him!

Far, far below: Jopling's arms and legs flail as he disappears down into the deepest reaches of the chasm. M. Gustave says proudly in elation:

Well done, Zero!

M. Gustave looks greatly relieved as he continues to hang precariously and his fingers stiffen toward frostbite. Zero gasps for an instant, then thrusts his arms down, stretching, to seize M. Gustave by the wrists.

Cut to:

A binocular shot of Zero dragging M. Gustave back up onto solid ground. They dust the snow off their bodies and catch their breath.

Henckels' voice shouts over a megaphone:

HENCKELS
(*out of shot*)

Halt!

M. Gustave and Zero look across the hillside to the next slope. A hundred advancing troops hurry toward them, descending swiftly. The tiny figure of Henckels at the head of the squadron continues forcefully:

Gustave H.! You're a fugitive from justice! Do not attempt to flee! Surrender lawfully, and I personally vouchsafe your fair treatment! Repeat: do not attempt to flee!

M. Gustave turns to Zero. Zero says, unsure:

ZERO

What do you think?

M. GUSTAVE
(*weary*)

I don't know. I'd rather jump off this cliff right now than go
back to fucking prison.

*M. Gustave looks lost and tired. Zero stares at him. He nods. He says
calmly:*

ZERO

I say we steal that sick maniac's motorcycle, go fetch
Agatha, take back 'Boy with Apple', and head for the
Maltese Riviera, once and for all.

M. Gustave's face lightens. He is moved and deeply impressed.

M. GUSTAVE

Very good! You're *so* extraordinary, Zero. Thank you.
(*Gravely.*) A moment of silence in memoriam of a devoted
servant killed violently during the conduct of his duties.

*M. Gustave and Zero stare solemnly into space for about five seconds.
Bloodhounds bark in the far distance. Zero says quietly:*

ZERO

Goodbye, Serge.

*M. Gustave nods suddenly. He and Zero break into a sprint, race over
to the motorcycle, and jump on. Zero kick-starts the engine, and M.
Gustave, on the rear fender, hangs on tightly as they rumble away
down the icy road.*

Cut to:

*Henckels watching from the distance. He lowers his binoculars. He
looks worried.*

MR. MOUSTAFA
(*voice-over*)

The war began at midnight.

Cut to:

*M. Gustave and Zero winding along the highway. Zero yells back over
his shoulder:*

What's it like, by the way? The Maltese Riviera!

M. GUSTAVE
(*pause*)
Charming, really! The weather's exquisite. The local cuisine is simple but excellent! The people are warm, kind, honest! Rather dusky-complexioned. You'll fit right in, actually!

Zero nods, pleased.

Title:

24 HOURS LATER

Montage:

Various white-gloved hands in action: one rings a bell on the concierge desk with a quick tap. Another slips an envelope into a message box. Another picks up a room key off a hook. Another forcefully shakes a cocktail-shaker full of ice.

MR. MOUSTAFA
(*voice-over*)
Pffeifelstad fell by lunch under heavy shelling, and the Zig-Zags surged across the long, western border. The Lutz Blitz would last all winter.

Insert:

A Martini glass. The drink is poured neatly – then stirred with a 'Z-Z' swizzle-stick.

MR. MOUSTAFA
(*voice-over*)
High Command advanced to Nebelsbad.

INT. LOBBY. DAY

The hotel is busier than ever, and every man in the room is in uniform. 'Z-Z' symbols are plastered across every conceivable surface.

Agatha comes in the front doors carrying a tall stack of pink cardboard pastry-boxes. A soldier seated at a small desk blocking the entrance looks up from his ledger book. He frowns. Agatha explains:

128

AGATHA

Compliments of Herr Mendl. For the Executive Staff.

Agatha takes a smaller box off the top of the stack and sets it down in front of the soldier. The soldier hesitates. He opens the box and sees inside: one Courtesan au chocolat. He looks back up to Agatha, hopeful. She nods. He signals for her to proceed.

An officer with a crew-cut mans the concierge desk. A badge on his chest reads: 'Military Concierge'. He is M. Chuck. Mr. Mosher stands beside him taking notes while he dictates orders:

M. CHUCK

General Stieglitz requests a garden-view sitting room with an extra roll-away. Let's put him in the Duke Leopold Suite. Secretary Woroniecki's office cabled. He's checking-in a day early (rooms 401–2–3). Tell Tactical Logistics we're moving them to a standard-double on the third floor.

MR. MOSHER
(*skeptical*)
They'll need more space than that.

Mr. Mosher points to a group of four soldiers carrying a ping-pong table through the lobby. Agatha waits calmly while they pass. She pauses, looks left and right, then ducks through a curtain below a sign that reads: STAFF ONLY. *She dashes up a staircase.*

Cut to:

The storage pantry adjacent to the vault. Agatha comes in and sets aside her boxes. She immediately stands on a chair and runs her hand along the top of a picture rail near the ceiling. She finds a brass key. She unlocks the outer door of the vault and slides it open – revealing the inner one (which has a combination lock).

Agatha reaches into her pocket and withdraws Zero's handwritten square of tissue-paper and a small magnifying glass. She squints and studies the tiny document. She quickly spins the dial and opens the door.

Agatha whips the fur stole off the radiator.

She pulls out the wrapped painting.

She tucks the package under her arm, exits the vault, and relocks the doors.

INT. VAN. DAY

The entrance to the hotel. 'Z-Z' banners hang from every awning. A dozen Zubrowkian flags wave and rustle in a row. Crests, heralds, and insignias are displayed in vitrines, doors, and windows. A chanting platoon marches up the promenade, and a soldier in a pilot's cap sits smoking a cigarette on top of a parked tank next to the funicular.

M. Gustave and Zero wait, tense, in a parked delivery truck with 'Mendl's' painted in delicate, pink cursive across the side. The engine idles. Zero is at the wheel. He and M. Gustave both wear white caps and aprons. M. Gustave says, deeply disgusted, as he stares at the new ornamentation:

> M. GUSTAVE
> The beginning of the end of the end of the beginning –
> has begun. A sad finale played, off-key, on a broken down
> saloon piano in the outskirts of a forgotten ghost town. I'd
> rather not bear witness to such blasphemy.

> ZERO
> Me, neither.

> M. GUSTAVE
> (*elegiac*)
> The Grand Budapest has become a troops' barracks. I shall
> never cross its threshold again in my lifetime.

> ZERO
> Me, neither.

> M. GUSTAVE
> (*on a roll*)
> Never again shall –

> ZERO
> (*alarmed*)
> Actually, I think we might be going in right now, after all.

Zero points to a long, silver limousine (last seen parked in front of the

Desgoffe und Taxis mansion in Lutz) as it pulls up the drive and stops between the Mendl's van and the entrance to the hotel. A liveried chauffeur jumps out and opens one of the back doors.

Dmitri emerges.

M. Gustave and Zero crouch down low in their seats. M. Gustave whispers with contempt:

M. GUSTAVE

Dmitri.

ZERO
(whispering, worried)

Agatha.

M. Gustave and Zero watch as: Marguerite, Laetizia, and Carolina exit from the other side of the car, and an eager team of bellboys springs into action collecting their numerous bags and suitcases out of the trunk and off the roof-rack of the vehicle.

Cut to:

Agatha poking her head back into the lobby from behind the curtain.

She starts toward the front door but pauses as she sees:

Dmitri and his sisters. They enter and are immediately greeted by M. Chuck. A large assembly of maids and footman stand in a row at attention to receive these distinguished guests.

> M. CHUCK
>
> Good evening, Mr. Desgoffe und Taxis. I'm M. Chuck. We've booked you and your sisters in the King Ferdinand Suite.

Dmitri shakes hands coolly. As M. Chuck introduces himself to Marguerite, Laetizia, and Carolina, Dmitri spots Agatha. He stares at her, curious. She looks back at him, uneasy. He focuses on the package under her arm. She turns away and walks quickly deeper into the lobby. Dmitri frowns.

> M. CHUCK
>
> General von Shrecker personally asked me to make sure –

> DMITRI
> *(interrupting)*
>
> Excuse me.

Dmitri bolts into the room.

Agatha's eyes dart, searching for an escape route, as she zooms among the tables, couches, tea trays, officers, waiters, and bellboys.

At the concierge desk: Henckels looks up from signing the guest book. He watches Agatha pass. He watches Dmitri grimly pursuing her. He looks intrigued.

Agatha bee-lines into the elevator. The elevator operator looks to her and waits. She hesitates. She names the top floor:

> AGATHA
>
> Six.

Just as the elevator operator starts to shut the gate – a voice commands him:

> DMITRI
> *(out of shot)*
>
> Hold it.

The elevator operator pauses. Dmitri enters and stands next to Agatha.

He stares ahead into space and repeats:

Six.

The elevator operator slams the door.

Henckels watches from across the lobby. He says to Anatole:

HENCKELS

Get M. Chuck.

Anatole nods and dashes away.

At the front door: M. Gustave and Zero stride into the building holding two tall stacks of pink, cardboard pastry-boxes. They stop. M. Gustave says warmly:

M. GUSTAVE

Compliments of Herr Mendl.

The soldier at the desk blocking the entrance looks up. He is halfway through his Courtesan au chocolat. *He has butter-cream on his moustache.*

Cut to:

Henckels on his way up the steps followed by M. Chuck. They stop at the next floor, look up and down the corridor, then continue climbing.

Cut to:

Mr. Mosher staring, curious; Herr Becker watching, surprised; and Anatole gaping, mouth open, at: M. Gustave and Zero crossing speedily through the center of the lobby with their stacked boxes, looking around in every direction as they go. They arrive at the closed elevator. A lobby boy stands next to it. He has curly hair and looks to be about sixteen. He is Otto.

M. GUSTAVE

Have you seen a pastry girl with a package under her arm in the last minute and a half?

OTTO

Yep! She just got on the elevator with Mr. Desgoffe und Taxis.

133

M. GUSTAVE
(*irritated*)

Thank you.

M. Gustave and Zero look up at the wall. Something is gnawing at them both.

Insert:

The needle above the elevator entrance. It climbs past 'Four' toward 'Five'.

M. Gustave and Zero start to dash away – but Zero stops short and turns back. He says quickly to Otto:

ZERO

I'm sorry. Who are you?

OTTO
(*hesitates*)

Otto, sir. The new lobby boy.

ZERO
(*sharply*)

Well, you haven't been trained properly, Otto. A lobby boy never provides information of that kind. You're a *stone wall*. Understood?

OTTO
(*anxious*)

Yes, sir.

M. Gustave and Zero exchange a quick look: well-handled. They run.

INT. ELEVATOR. DAY

As the lift ascends:

Dmitri casts a sideways look to Agatha. She stares ahead and avoids his eyes. He looks away.

Agatha casts a sideways look to Dmitri. He snaps his head suddenly to look at her. She turns away again immediately, stricken.

Dmitri reaches out toward Agatha. She retreats further into the corner.

134

He touches the package under her arm with his long fingers and peels back the edge of the wrapping-paper – revealing a white hand holding a golden apple. He says quietly:

DMITRI

Pretty picture.

Agatha does not respond. They come to a stop, and the elevator operator opens the gate.

ELEVATOR OPERATOR

Sixth floor.

Neither Agatha nor Dmitri move. Silence. The elevator operator turns around slightly to look at them.

Agatha exits. The elevator operator starts to close the door, but Dmitri holds up a finger. He follows Agatha. The gate closes behind him.

Agatha walks swiftly but calmly down the long corridor. She looks back. Dmitri walks behind her, equally swiftly and significantly more calmly, thirty feet back. Agatha turns a corner.

Dmitri cracks his knuckles as he continues. He clears his throat. He turns the corner now, himself, and sees:

Agatha running as fast as she can, already sixty feet ahead, nearly at the end of the corridor. She looks back again as she disappears around the next corner.

Dmitri breaks into a full sprint. In five seconds, he reaches the end of the hallway. He stops and looks down the next corridor.

It is empty. Pause.

At the far end: a pair of doors labeled SERVICE ELEVATOR *slide open. M. Gustave and Zero stand inside it with their stacked boxes. Dmitri's eyes widen. He shouts:*

DMITRI

Where's 'Boy with Apple'?

M. GUSTAVE
(*pause*)
None of your goddamn business!

DMITRI
(*hesitates*)
I'm going to blast your candy-ass once and for all right
now!

*Dmitri instantly leans down, lifts up his trouser leg, and draws a
small-calibre handgun from a strap under his sock. He fires.*

*M. Gustave and Zero throw their boxes in every direction and duck to
the sides of the elevator. Dmitri fires again. Bullets ricochet.*

*A door opens halfway down the corridor. An officer wearing his
uniform tunic but no trousers looks out at Dmitri, alerted, with a
Luger pistol in his hand.*

OFFICER
Drop your weapon!

*Dmitri fires three more times into the service elevator. The officer fires
back at Dmitri. Dmitri ducks behind a room-service cart and quickly
reloads. More doors open up and down the corridor, and more armed
officers in various states of dress/undress look out.*

*Dmitri pops up again and resumes his barrage. All the officers open
fire at once, shooting, apparently at random, in both directions.
Henckels appears suddenly at the top of the stairs with his own
firearm drawn. M. Chuck hurries behind him. Henckels ducks down
low and screams:*

HENCKELS
Cease fire! Cease fire! Stop it!

*The gunfire pauses. Everyone remains poised for the next volley.
Henckels hollers:*

Who's shooting who?

DMITRI
(*behind his barricade*)
That's Gustave H.! The escaped murderer and art thief!
I've got him cornered!

*M. Gustave and Zero remain tucked against the walls on the floor of
the service elevator. M. Gustave yells, enraged:*

M. GUSTAVE

That's Dmitri Desgoffe und Taxis! He's responsible for the killings of Deputy Kovacs, Serge X. and his club-footed sister, plus his own mother!

HENCKELS
(*hesitates*)
*No*body move! *Every*body's under arrest!

There is a loud creak, then a crashing bang. M. Chuck squints at an open window in a small alcove across from him.

M. CHUCK

Who's out the window?

Zero looks to M. Gustave. He says, under his breath:

ZERO

Agatha!

Zero sprints out of the service elevator and races up the corridor. Dmitri starts shooting again. The entire group opens fire once more. Zero runs, crouched, with his hands over his head, and ducks into the alcove. His head thrusts out the window. He looks down.

Cut to:

Agatha swinging by one hand from a broken trellis off the end of a terrace three flights below. She hangs onto the wrapped painting with her other hand. She notices something on it and frowns.

Insert:

The dangling package. A section of the wrapping paper has torn away, and the corner of a pale-pink envelope is visible pasted to the back of the picture.

Zero stares down at Agatha, horrified. He mutters to himself:

ZERO

310-*bis*! (*Shouting to Agatha.*) Hang on! Here I come!

Zero races back through the hail of bullets. He darts past Henckels and down the stairwell. He descends three flights. He crosses the corridor and stops in front of a door labeled '310-bis'. A sign on the knob reads: 'Do Not Disturb'.

Zero hesitates an instant.

He raps briskly, retreats back across the corridor, lowers his shoulder, and charges with all his strength.

Just as he reaches the door, it swings open to reveal a small, bearded man in a long nightgown. He sidesteps Zero.

Zero stumbles full speed through the sitting room and out the wide-open terrace doors. He slams against the balcony railing and flips over it. Agatha releases the package and grabs Zero's shirt as he somersaults over her.

Zero's weight jerks Agatha down with a jolt. They fall together.

Four floors down, Zero and Agatha punch through the canvas roof of the back of the Mendl's van and disappear inside. Silence.

INT. VAN. DAY

Zero sits up among the chaotic pile of scattered and upturned pink, cardboard pastry-boxes. He gasps and digs for Agatha. She surfaces.

>   ZERO
> Agatha! Are you all right?

>   AGATHA
>   (*dazed*)
>   I think so.

Zero embraces Agatha. He kisses her passionately. He looks into her eyes. She says, woozy:

>   Something's on the back of the picture.

>   ZERO
>   (*confused*)
> What?

Agatha holds a piece of the torn and crumbled wrapping paper. She and Zero both look straight up.

Cut to:

Zero and Agatha's point-of-view through the hole punched in the roof of the van. Seven floors up, M. Gustave, Henckels, and M. Chuck lean out the window staring down at them, frozen, while other officers lean out other windows all across the facade. Four floors up, 'Boy with Apple', unwrapped, hangs upside-down from a wire below the balcony. It swings gently.

Insert:

The painting, upside-down. A pair of hands flips it over to reveal the pale-pink envelope on the reverse.

Title:

PART 6:
'THE SECOND COPY OF THE SECOND WILL'

INT. DINING ROOM. DAY

The entire, vast assembly of officers and soldiers stands crowded, murmuring, around a table in the restaurant where M. Gustave, Zero, and Dmitri, all in handcuffs, sit across from Henckels. Agatha stands behind Zero. Marguerite, Laetizia, and Carolina stand behind Dmitri. M. Chuck stands behind Henckels.

Henckels carefully peels the envelope loose from the back of the canvas. He slits it open with a pocket knife and removes a handwritten letter on pale-pink paper. He skims it, then looks to M. Gustave.

> MR. MOUSTAFA
> (*voice-over*)
> She left everything to M. Gustave, of course.

INT. COURTROOM. DAY

M. Gustave on the witness stand. He wears his concierge uniform and is immaculate. The jury listens, enraptured by his testimony. The judge sniffs the air. He looks irritated.

> MR. MOUSTAFA
> (*voice-over*)
> The mansion, known as Schloss Lutz; the factories, which produced weapons, medicine, and textiles; an important newspaper syndicate; and (perhaps you've already deduced) this very 'institution' – the Grand Budapest Hotel.

Zero, Agatha, Herr Becker, Mr. Mosher, and Anatole watch, entertained, from the gallery.

Insert:

The front page of the Trans-Alpine Yodel. *Headline:* CLEARED OF ALL CHARGES. *A photograph shows M. Gustave with the entire staff posing in front of the Grand Budapest. A column below the fold reads, 'Son of Murdered Countess Disappears without Trace.'*

Cut to:

Zero behind the concierge desk. He now wears a uniform identical to M. Gustave's. He rattles off instructions to Mr. Mosher, Herr Becker, Anatole, and M. Chuck.

> MR. MOUSTAFA
> (*voice-over*)
> He anointed me his successor; and, as the war continued, I served my adopted country from the narrow desk still found against the wall in the next room.

Across the lobby, M. Gustave sits drinking a cocktail with a beautiful, begemmed, ninety-year-old woman. His hand rests on her thigh.

> He was the same as his disciples: insecure, vain, superficial, blonde, needy. In the end, he was even rich.

EXT. MOUNTAIN RANGE. DAY

The facade of the Grand Budapest at sunset. The camera glides along the path through the plot of edelweiss and buttercups.

> MR. MOUSTAFA
> (*voice-over*)
> He did not succeed, however, in growing old – nor did my darling Agatha. She and our infant son would be killed two years later by the Prussian *grippe*. (An absurd little disease. Today, we treat it in a single week; but, in those days, many millions died.)

The camera comes to a stop as it reveals the view from the iron-lattice terrace over the crevasse alongside the cascade.

Zero and Agatha hold hands while M. Gustave reads from a Bible, officiating. The other witnesses are the staff of the hotel and the concierges of the Society of the Crossed Keys.

INT. TRAIN COMPARTMENT. DAY

A first-class state room on the express to Lutz. M. Gustave, Zero, and Agatha each hold a glass of chilled, white wine.

> MR. MOUSTAFA
> (*voice-over*)
> On the first day of the occupation, the morning the independent state of Zubrowka officially ceased to exist, we traveled with M. Gustave to Lutz.

M. Gustave checks the color of the wine in the light. It is excellent. Pause.

> M. GUSTAVE
> In answer to your earlier question, by the way: of course.

Zero looks slightly puzzled. M. Gustave explains, aside, to Agatha:

> M. GUSTAVE
> Zero asked me about my humble beginnings in the hotel trade. (*To Zero and Agatha both.*) I was, perhaps, for a time, considered the best lobby boy we'd ever *had* at the Grand Budapest. I think I can say that. *This* one – (*pointing to Zero*) finally surpassed me. Although, I must say, he had an exceptional teacher.

> ZERO
> (*with great affection*)
> Truly.

> AGATHA
> (*reciting*)
> 'Whence came these two, radiant, celestial brothers, united, for an instant, as they crossed the stratosphere of our starry window? One from the East, and one from the West.'

> M. GUSTAVE
> (*impressed*)
> *Very* good.

M. Gustave kisses Agatha's hand. Zero frowns.

ZERO

Don't flirt with her. (*Suddenly.*) Why are we stopping at a
barley field again?

*The train has, in fact, again come to a halt in the middle of nowhere –
but, this time, outside the window, there are tanks, trucks, and a
hundred soldiers in black uniforms with long coats. M. Gustave, Zero,
and Agatha stare out at them, uneasy.*

M. GUSTAVE

I find these black uniforms very drab. I suppose they're
meant to frighten people, but –

*Three soldiers appear in the compartment doorway. They are stocky,
thick-necked, and armed with carbine rifles. M. Gustave says with his
usual air of fancy-meeting-you-here:*

M. GUSTAVE

Well, hello there, chaps. We were just talking about you.

SOLDIER I
(*blankly*)

Documents, please.

M. GUSTAVE

With pleasure – as always.

*M. Gustave and Agatha withdraw their passports and present them to
the soldier. The soldier flips through them.*

M. GUSTAVE

You're the first of the enemy forces to whom we've been
formally introduced. How do you do?

*The soldier ignores this comment. He returns the passports to M.
Gustave and Agatha and looks to Zero. Zero nervously hands him his
little scrap of paper. The soldier frowns and studies it. M. Gustave
smiles. He says lightly:*

M. GUSTAVE

Plus ça change, am I right? (*To the soldier.*) That's a
Migratory Visa with Stage Three Worker Status, darling.
Read this.

M. Gustave hands the soldier Henckels' special document. The soldier shows it to his associates. They confer rapidly at a whisper. There is some debate. Before M. Gustave can work his magic – the soldier rips the special document to shreds.

Pause.

M. Gustave looks to Zero. Zero and Agatha are both stunned and frightened. M. Gustave seems to smile very slightly, reassuring them, and somehow sends a sincere, private message:

> M. GUSTAVE
>
> Good luck.

M. Gustave's jaw hardens. He pegs his glass of wine at the soldier, shattering it, and explodes:

> You filthy, goddamn, pock-marked, fascist assholes!

M. Gustave is instantly on his feet, tussling. Zero jumps up to intervene, trying to calm everyone down – and is immediately bashed in the face with the stock of a rifle and dropped to the floor, out cold. M. Gustave shouts and struggles. Agatha screams.

> MR. MOUSTAFA
> (*voice-over*)
> There *are* still faint glimmers of civilization left in this barbaric slaughterhouse that was once known as humanity.

INT. CORRIDOR. DAY

The three soldiers whisk M. Gustave, now in handcuffs, out of the compartment and manhandle him down the length of the coach while he shouts furiously, berating them:

> M. GUSTAVE
> I give you my word: I'll see all three of you dishonorably discharged, locked-up in the stockade, and *hanged* by sundown! (*Screaming in rage.*) Where is your commanding officer?

Cut to:

Zero with his head out the window of the once-again speeding train.

A significant volume of blood runs from his forehead around his eye and down into his shirt collar, soaked deep red. He clutches his little scrap of paper in his fist. The wind rustles against his neck. His mouth is open. His face is frozen. Tears stream down his cheeks.

> MR. MOUSTAFA
> *(voice-over, re: 'glimmers of civilization')*
> He was one of them. What more is there to say?

Agatha, also in tears, pulls Zero back inside.

Cut to:

The dining room. Mr. Moustafa and the author sit in front of their desserts: Courtesans au chocolat. They are the last remaining guests in the giant restaurant. A waiter sets places for breakfast at tables in the background.

Two glasses of sweet wine are served. Mr. Moustafa and the author sip them. The author asks gently:

> AUTHOR
> What happened in the end?

> MR. MOUSTAFA
> *(shrugs)*
> In the end, they shot him. (*Pause.*) So it all went to me.

Mr. Moustafa smiles sadly. He and the author begin to eat their confections in silence. They appear to enjoy them very much.

INT. LOBBY. NIGHT

The room is deserted, and the lights have been dimmed. Mr. Moustafa and the author wait at the concierge desk. It is not occupied.

> AUTHOR
> *(voice-over)*
> After dinner, we went to collect the keys to our rooms – but M. Jean had abandoned his post.

Mr. Moustafa looks around. He shrugs. He says, bittersweet:

> MR. MOUSTAFA
> I expect he's forgotten all about us.

Mr. Moustafa winks at the author and slips around behind the concierge desk.

> AUTHOR
> (*voice-over*)
> In recent years, of course, such properties and holdings as the Grand Budapest had with very few exceptions become – common property.

Mr. Moustafa takes great pleasure as he: opens a drawer and tidies up its contents slightly; pulls a stack of envelopes out of a slot, flips through them, and hands one to the author; straightens 'Boy with Apple' slightly; then takes two keys off their hooks.

> AUTHOR
> (*voice-over*)
> While the precise terms of his negotiation with the new government had never been announced, the result was an open secret: Zero Moustafa had traded a great and important fortune in exchange for one costly, unprofitable, doomed hotel. Why?

Insert:

The author's room key as Mr. Moustafa places it onto the desk. It is labeled M. GUSTAVE SUITE.

> AUTHOR
> (*voice-over*)
> Was it merely sentimental?

Mr. Moustafa holds the author by the arm with two hands as the author walks him the length of the room to the elevator.

> It was quite forward of me and a bit out of character, but I felt I must know – for my health, I suppose. I took the plunge.

Cut to:

One minute later. Mr. Moustafa and the author stand at the entrance to the elevator facing each other. Silence. The author says suddenly, slightly worried:

AUTHOR

Forgive me for asking. I hope I haven't upset you.

MR. MOUSTAFA
(*dismissing it*)

Of course, not.

AUTHOR
(*long pause*)

Is it simply your last connection to that – vanished world?
His world, if you will?

MR. MOUSTAFA
(*doubtful*)

His world?

Mr. Moustafa considers this. He shakes his head slowly.

No, I don't think so. You see, we shared a vocation. It
wouldn't have been necessary. He's *always* with me.
(*Pause.*) No, the hotel – I keep for Agatha.

*Mr. Moustafa pulls up his lapel slightly and shows the author Agatha's
crossed-keys pendant pinned to his jacket. He hides it away again.*

MR. MOUSTAFA

We were happy here. For a little while.

*The author nods solemnly. Mr. Moustafa presses a button to call the
elevator. It immediately opens. He starts to enter – but puts up his
hand to hold the door as he stops, turns back, and says:*

To be frank, I think *his* world had vanished long before he
ever entered it – but, I will say: he certainly sustained the
illusion with a marvelous grace! (*Pause.*) Are you going up?

AUTHOR
(*politely*)

No, I'll sit for a little while. Good night.

MR. MOUSTAFA

Good night.

*Mr. Moustafa steps inside. He presses a button and the doors close. The
author stands still, staring into space. He sniffs the air. He smiles sadly.*

AUTHOR
(*voice-over*)

The next week, I sailed for a cure in South America and began a long, wandering journey abroad. I did not return to Europe for many years.

EXT. HOTEL. NIGHT

The entrance at midnight. A doorman sweeps the steps below the front door. Only one room's light is illuminated: a little window at the far edge of the top floor.

AUTHOR
(*voice-over*)

It *was* an enchanting old ruin – but I never managed to see it again.

The light goes out.

Cut to:

The lobby. The author sits alone in an armchair in the deserted room writing in a small notebook.

Cut to:

The study. The author (at seventy-five) sits in an armchair writing in an identical small notebook. The six-year-old boy plays with an army of metal soldiers on the floor beside him.

Cut to:

The park. The girl in the trench-coat and beret sits on a bench near the statue of the author. She is just finishing the final chapter of:

THE GRAND BUDAPEST HOTEL

The Grand Budapest Hotel

CHARACTER SKETCHES BY JUMAN MALOUF

Young Author

M. Jean

M. Gustave H.   Madame D.

Zero   Mr. Moustafa

Agatha

Henckels

Dmitri Jopling

Deputy Kovacs   Ludwig